THE INTELLIGENT DESIGN OF JENNY CHOW

AN INSTANT MESSAGE WITH EXCITABLE MUSIC

BY **ROLIN JONES**

DRAMATISTS
PLAY SERVICE
INC.

For
Debra Grieb

THE INTELLIGENT DESIGN OF JENNY CHOW was originally performed as a collaborative workshop project at the Yale School of Drama. It was produced by Mark Bly. The director was Kara-Lynn Vaeni. The cast was as follows:

JENNIFER MARCUS .... Jennifer Lim
MR. MARCUS / MR. ZHANG .... Kevin Rich
PRESTON / TERRENCE / COL. HUBBARD /
DR. YAKUNIN / VOICE OF COMPUTER
TRANSLATOR .... Adam O'Byrne
ADELE HARTWICK / MS. ZHANG .... Kristen Fiorella
TODD / A BOY .... Ryan King
JENNY CHOW .... Keiko Yamamoto

THE INTELLIGENT DESIGN OF JENNY CHOW premiered at South Coast Repertory Theater (Martin Benson and David Emmes, Artistic Directors) in Costa Mesa, California, in April 2003. It was directed by David Chambers; the set design was by Christopher Barecca; the costume design was by Dunya Ramicova; the lighting design was by Chris Perry; the sound design was by David Budries; and the production stage manager was Jamie A. Tucker. The cast was as follows:

JENNIFER MARCUS .... Melody Butiu
MR. MARCUS / MR. ZHANG .... William Francis McGuire
PRESTON / TERRENCE / COL. HUBBARD /
DR. YAKUNIN / VOICE OF COMPUTER
TRANSLATOR .... J.D. Cullum
ADELE HARTWICK / MS. ZHANG .... Linda Gehringer
TODD / A BOY .... Daniel Blinkoff
JENNY CHOW .... April Hong

THE INTELLIGENT DESIGN OF JENNY CHOW was produced at the Atlantic Theater Company (Neil Pepe, Artistic Director) in New York City, opening in September 2005. It was directed by Jackson Gay; the set design was by Takeshi Kata; the costume design was by Jenny Mannis; the lighting design was by Tyler Micoleau; the sound design was by Daniel Baker; the original music was composed by Matthew Suttor; and the production stage manager was Robyn Henry. The cast was as follows:

JENNIFER MARCUS .... Julienne Hanzelka Kim
MR. MARCUS / MR. ZHANG .... Michael Cullen
PRESTON / TERRENCE / COL. HUBBARD /
DR. YAKUNIN / VOICE OF COMPUTER
TRANSLATOR .... Remy Auberjonois
ADELE HARTWICK / MS. ZHANG .... Linda Gehringer
TODD / A BOY .... Ryan King
JENNY CHOW .... Eunice Wong

AUTHOR'S NOTE

Live theater, as practiced by this author, is an act of thievery. The pages bound here within are the product of six different productions, five directors, four dramaturgs, thirty-two actors, twenty-five designers and a countless number of production staff, writing mentors, and dear friends who contributed their unique and considerable gifts toward the creation of something I will, ridiculously, get sole credit for. It's a complete scam. For posterity and a more transparent future I say — thank you all, every last one of you. Know I stole only your best ideas.

I wish to thank the following folks for their dramaturgical and/ or spiritual guidance; Lynn, Mark, Ruth, Robert, Connie, Marcus, Jami, Sarah, Kate, Rey, Ezra, Roberto, Jason, Zakkiyah, Leslie, Tim, David C., Kara, Jen, Jerry, Emily S., Kirsten, Seema, Jackson, Christine, Christie, Christian, Jackson (Did I mention Jackson?), Carson, Ken M., Janet, Todd, David G., David M., Elizabeth B., Chris T., Larry S., Emily Jane, Melissa, Brian, Kim, the Family Bundy, the Family Flynn, the Family Finkel, the Family Lyons, the Brothers Rothstein, Larry, Bob, Ken H., Joan B., Tom, Leerhuber, Maestro (RIP), Maverick, Alisha K., Karen H., Mary Joan, Elizabeth Clare Douglas, and Carol Linder.

More to the future, for those of you warped enough to produce this, allow me two suggestions. 1) Please consider carefully the borderline-precious subtitle, "An instant message with excitable music." Any time you feel lost return to it. That is what the thing is. And with this in mind, think seriously about using the sound design and original music by Daniel Baker and Matthew Suttor. Sound and music, as practiced by this author, is text. To that I mean, the play is underwritten where music exists and overwritten where there is none. It is the river Jennifer Marcus floats on and the thread for a purposefully patchwork quilt. Consider their work as integral as the actor's dialogue and compensate them a fair wage. They are scrawny men and need their vitamins. 2) If you have a choice between equal male and female directing candidates, keep in mind the play was written by a white dude from the San Fernando Valley. It could use all the female energy it can get.

With all that said, I offer you a map. Extraordinary cartographers have held it before you, but there is much uncharted water. All other problems, call the landlord.

Yours sincerely,
Rolin Jones

CHARACTERS

JENNIFER MARCUS, 22, Asian-American

MR. MARCUS / MR. ZHANG, early 50s

PRESTON / TERRENCE / COL. HUBBARD / DR. YAKUNIN / VOICE OF COMPUTER TRANSLATOR, late 20s, early 30s

ADELE HARTWICK / MS. ZHANG, late 40s, early 50s

TODD / A BOY, early 20s

JENNY CHOW, early 20s, Asian-American

PLACE

A second-story bedroom, Calabasas, California.

TIME

Now, right now.

THE INTELLIGENT
DESIGN OF JENNY CHOW

ACT ONE

We hear intense, percussive music, suggesting an air of conspiracy. We see Jennifer Marcus in her bedroom, her face illuminated by a laptop computer screen. There should be some clutter — a spray can of disinfectant, some empty boxes and tubular cardboard. She is dressed without concern for her appearance except for a beautiful silk scarf wrapped around her neck. She is typing at a breathtaking speed. She looks right above the computer screen at the audience.

JENNIFER MARCUS. *(To the audience.)* Dr. Yakunin says I can trust you. But just because you have a reference like that doesn't mean we're going to work together or that I don't have other options, okay? Let's just say, I've done some research and I know your competition. Ramirez? Bloomstedt? Okay? So I'm not going to take a lot of clandestine bullshit, alright? *(We hear a "blip" noise from the computer. To the audience.)* Good. 'Cause I don't want you to think I'm some sort of bitch, okay? I'm not. I'm a lot of fun. Okay, so, this is what I know about you. You were a decorated Army Ranger mostly assigned to search-and-rescue missions. You've been a freelance bounty hunter ever since you retired and you work alone. You have citizenship with five different countries under three different names. You have a near sixty-percent capture rate which I'm told in your line of work is something close to astonishing and which makes me think, you have some serious low expectations for yourself. Okay soooo, you've never been married but you like prostitutes, although you might want to avoid the young ones in the greater DC area considering the amount of sperm you donated as an undergrad at Georgetown, okay? *(She hits herself in the head. To the audience.)* Wait, I wasn't supposed to say that. That was my joke to Todd. (Why am I talking about Todd?) I'll tell you about Todd later. That was stupid, 'cause hey, you know, I've had dreams of sleeping with my dad, who hasn't? But they're never sexy and it's fucking gross, you know? Okay, weird. I'm a weirdo. Soooo we got off track for a sec, and now we're gonna get back on it. *(She sprays the computer with disinfectant. To the audience.)* I see you've made some creative investments in the last year. Money in Chilean bonds, a racehorse named "El Jefe." In your line of work I guess you just don't have time to master the basics of money management. Laughing out loud!

VOICE OF MR. MARCUS. Jennifer!

JENNIFER MARCUS. *(To the audience.)* I guess you have to trust people. That's what Dr. Yakunin always says. He also said you were cute. And I think he's right, you know, looking at your picture, cute for a forty-year-old. And much more attractive than Bloomstedt or Ramirez. I mean, Ramirez? Fucking gross, okay. *(Mr. Marcus appears, talking through the door.)*

MR. MARCUS. Jennifer, honey.

JENNIFER MARCUS. *(To the audience.)* Be right back. *(The music abruptly cuts out. Turns around.)* I'm not here.

MR. MARCUS. I've made dinner.

JENNIFER MARCUS. *(Turning back.)* I'm really busy, Dad.

MR. MARCUS. I made your favorite

JENNIFER MARCUS. *(To the audience.)* Okay, I'm back.

MR. MARCUS. I made chili dogs!

JENNIFER MARCUS. *(Annoyed.)* That's *your* favorite, Dad.

MR. MARCUS. I double-cooked them.

JENNIFER MARCUS. *(Trying to ignore her dad.)* There's a lot to tell you and I don't have a lot of time. I really screwed up bad. I need your help.

MR. MARCUS. Twice-cooked dogs smothered in the old man's con carne.

JENNIFER MARCUS. *(To the audience.)* First thing, I'm a bit concerned about security. The firewall in your system is at least a year old, it's almost unforgivable. I'm forwarding you a program I designed myself. You need to install it now, okay? *(We hear a "bling" noise from the computer.)*

MR. MARCUS. Your mother's gonna want to know when you're coming out.

JENNIFER MARCUS. *(To Mr. Marcus.)* Adele's not coming back and you know it.

MR. MARCUS. That's not true. We're both very worried about you.

JENNIFER MARCUS. Give it a rest, Dad.

MR. MARCUS. Say, there's a big fire in Chatsworth. We got a good view. A real scorcher! *(Jennifer holds up an X-ray.)*

JENNIFER MARCUS. *(To the audience.)* I want to thank you for overnighting me your dental records and hair sample. I know that's not usual protocol …

MR. MARCUS. Knock, knock, knock …

JENNIFER MARCUS. *(Turning around, loud.)* Adele doesn't give a shit about us. And you should be glad we're never gonna see her hateful fucking face again, how's that? Okay?

MR. MARCUS. I'll leave a plate by the stove. *(He exits.)*

JENNIFER MARCUS. *(To the audience.)* Okay, so this firewall is serious. Have you installed it yet? *(Pause.)* Yes, go ahead, check. *(A "hacker alert" noise from the computer. To the audience. Pause.)* Oh, that's cute. *(She types in something and the "alert" noise stops. She sprays the computer screen with disinfectant. We hear a "blip" noise from the computer. To the audience, annoyed.)* Yeah, I'm here. Installed? Goooood. You never know which one of the big boys might be listening in, right? CIA? NSA? We have to be careful, oh, and uh, yeah, we need to stick to what we're good at, okay? You find missing people, I do the computer stuff. Because next time we're in the middle of an IM and you try to break into my computer, I will send an f-bomb of kiddie porn that will bury itself in your hard drive and spam itself back to every sickfuck pedophile in the world currently under Interpol investigation, okay? I got viruses that can make you piss on yourself and I'm saying this, okay, not because I wouldn't have done the same thing, but because YOU REALLY NEED TO PAY ATTENTION. It's been three days since Jenny got loose. Every second counts. My encryption cannot be broken. Understand? *(We hear a "blip" noise from the computer. To the audience.)* Good. *(Jennifer puts on a voice-ID earpiece and starts pacing the room. As she talks she straightens pillows, realphabetizes her books, creates order or rearranges order. To the audience.)* Okay, so, here we go … my name is Jennifer Marcus and I was born in a village outside of Maigon-ko, China twenty-two years ago and … I'm a girl, duh, and I live in a gated community in Calabasas, California. One of the first things you're going to have to get used to is that I'm better than you. Wait, I'm not being conceited, not really, you know, there's a lot of baggage that comes with it. *(We hear a "blip" noise from the computer. To the audience.)* Not cabbage. Baggage. B-A-G-G-A-G-E. I'm using a headset voice identifier, there's some bugs still left in it, so try to stay with me as far as typos go, okay? Where was I? Right, well maybe not better, definitely not better, just more *active,* I guess. Oh yeah, and I'm rich. Not super rich. Just regular rich. I feel it's important that you know a little about me, and trust me, okay, you'll need it for the job. This isn't your average runaway case, okay? *(We hear a "boink" noise from the computer. To the audience.)* Christ. Can you hold on for a second? *(The music cuts out again. Jennifer types into the computer.)* Hello Preston. *(Lights up on Preston.)*

PRESTON. *(Slight Southern accent.)* Hi there, Miss Marcus. We just wondering how you doing on the orbital? *(She looks around her desk, grabs a strange gyroscope-like device, works on it with a small tool kit.)*

JENNIFER MARCUS. We're working on it right now, Preston, okay, I'm a little busy right now.

PRESTON. I know, but we were supposed to get it yesterday.

JENNIFER MARCUS. We're working on it, Preston.

PRESTON. I know. But Colonel Hubbard says these missiles ain't working right at all. We keep blowing up the wrong things.

JENNIFER MARCUS. It's right in front of me, right now, Preston.

PRESTON. We keep telling the missiles to go this way and they go that way and Colonel Hubbard says the guv'ment gonna stop our contract ...

JENNIFER MARCUS. I'm talking to someone else right now.

PRESTON. And if they stop our contract, I ain't got a job. And you know what kind of jobs they got out here in Gray, Georgia, Miss Marcus?

JENNIFER MARCUS. Preston ...

PRESTON. It's sewage. They got jobs at the sewage plant.

JENNIFER MARCUS. I've got to go, okay?

PRESTON. I don't wanna work sewage. That ain't good.

JENNIFER MARCUS. I'm working on it.

PRESTON. You working on it?

JENNIFER MARCUS. Goodbye, Preston.

PRESTON. O-kay, Miss Marcus, I'll tell the colonel. *(Lights down on Preston. Jennifer hits one key on the computer.)*

JENNIFER MARCUS. *(To the audience.)* Right, I'm back. That was Raytheon. Um, so I got a job reengineering obsolete missile components after I lost my job at the mall. Dr. Yakunin got me the job. I'm a bit of a mechanics whiz. Anyway, so my parents, right, met at a barbecue or whatever and they got married and they couldn't have a baby. I'm not sure whose pipes were plugged up, they don't talk about stuff like that and I don't really want to know, okay? Anyway, since I was a girl (and I guess that's not the best thing to be in China), my mother wrapped me in a silk scarf and gave me up for adoption. Six months later, my parents got on a plane to get me, so really, you know, thank God for Richard Nixon and all that. Anyway, I don't look anything like a Jennifer Marcus, but I kick ass and I've got big tits for an Asian, so whatever. *(Mrs. Adele Hartwick appears, pulling a suitcase and dialing a cell phone. To the audience.)* My mother, Ms. Adele Hartwick, has worked in the trade show industry for the last twenty years. *(Jennifer puts down the gyroscope, feels something stuck in her teeth.)*

ADELE HARTWICK. If there's a crack in the dam, Bob, that's where I'm at, that's how you can get ahold of me.

JENNIFER MARCUS. *(To the audience.)* She's with a very big company and as Chief Operating Officer, she has to travel a lot. *(Jennifer starts flossing her teeth, very meticulously.)*

ADELE HARTWICK. And I don't care what your relationship is with Stan, you turn me over on a conference call like you did today and you're out of luck. Because let me tell you, *I* don't think strategically?! *I'm* not a revenue producer?! That's bullcrap! *(Jennifer begins to brush her teeth and gargle mouthwash. She repeats this a number of times until it's almost uncomfortable.)* And I bled from my eye sockets to get your IBT shows squeezed into Javits, Bob, and your cluster still looks like shit, excuse me, so unless there's a miracle in the fourth quarter, your operating-costs-are-killing-me-story isn't gonna fly with Stan or Jim or Joe. Get some ethics, Bob, tell the truth. Take your load-in problems to Steve in Miami. *(Adele hangs up, dials again.)*

JENNIFER MARCUS. *(Spits, then to the audience.)* She travels Monday through Friday and comes home on the weekends, but mostly she doesn't get to come back. *(Jennifer starts flossing again.)*

ADELE HARTWICK. Laura, it's me. I'm looking at the monitor and my flight's been cancelled. I don't know why, that's your job! You get me another flight now because I'm *not* going into a seven o'clock meeting with Jay Atherton totally exhausted! Call me back when you've done your job. And this is the last time you book me into LaGuardia. It's bullcrap! *(Mr. Marcus appears in the back-*

ground with a radio, a pair of binoculars and a mobile phone.)

JENNIFER MARCUS. *(To the audience.)* My father was a fireman. But he hurt his back a long time ago, so really he was the one who raised me. At night, he likes to sit up on the deck with his police scanner and watch for fires. *(Jennifer checks her gums. Adele dials again.)*

MR. MARCUS. *(Into the phone.)* Hello, Carl?

JENNIFER MARCUS. Sometimes he'll call in fires before anyone knows about it.

MR. MARCUS. I think I see a brushfire beginning.

JENNIFER MARCUS. *(To the audience.)* He's got a lot of friends at the local firehouse.

MR. MARCUS. Could turn out to be a big one, Carl.

JENNIFER MARCUS. *(To the audience.)* My mother used to be named Adele Hartwick-Marcus.

MR. MARCUS. I think it's that hill by Topanga and Oxnard.

JENNIFER MARCUS. *(To the audience.)* Somewhere along the way, I think she went back to her maiden name. Some business decision or something.

MR. MARCUS. You should check it out, okay, Carl? Oops, think the wife's trying to beep in.

JENNIFER MARCUS. *(To the audience.)* I think it must've hurt my dad. But he never says anything about it. *(He hits a button on the phone.)*

MR. MARCUS. Hello?

ADELE HARTWICK. It's me. Flight got cancelled.

MR. MARCUS. Oh. Where are you?

ADELE HARTWICK. I'm in New York. What's going on there?

MR. MARCUS. Well, there's a fire in Woodland Hills. And a tomato truck overturned somewhere on the 101 …

ADELE HARTWICK. I'm having a helluva of a day here, Mark. I don't care about a tomato truck.

JENNIFER MARCUS. *(To the audience.)* I'm pretty much a complete disappointment to both my parents. We'll that's not true. Not my dad.

ADELE HARTWICK. Has she come out yet? Is she eating?

MR. MARCUS. No.

JENNIFER MARCUS. *(To the audience.)* He's not disappointed. He just has no expectations for me. Which I guess is kinda heart breaking if you dwell on it but it's a whole lot more liveable than my mother who's totally fed up with me.

16

ADELE HARTWICK. Starving herself now? Is that what I get to come home to?

MR. MARCUS. You did an awful thing, Adele.

JENNIFER MARCUS. *(To the audience.)* You see I have this dumb-ass thing called Obsessive-Compulsive Disorder. And it puts a lot of pressure on everyone in the house.

ADELE HARTWICK. Well, I'm upset, Mark.

JENNIFER MARCUS. *(To the audience.)* It started in high school with some mild Tourette's, not like I was going "fuckshitpussyfart" all the time. Just little stuff like, "Alrightyeah" or like "Okaywhatever" and no one noticed, you know.

ADELE HARTWICK. Mostly, I'm tired. But I'm upset. And I don't think I want to feel this way anymore.

JENNIFER MARCUS. *(To the audience.)* Because in addition to winning the National Science Fair, being president of the Rock Climbers Club and captain of the AcaDeca team, I was also the school mascot and people just figured I was a spaz or something.

MR. MARCUS. I think that fire is spreading.

ADELE HARTWICK. Everything's dissolving.

JENNIFER MARCUS. *(To the audience.)* See, what OCD really means is that it takes me a hell of a lot of time to do certain shit that most regular people can do in a minute.

ADELE HARTWICK. Christ. I'll call you later. *(Lights out on Mr. Marcus.)*

JENNIFER MARCUS. *(To the audience.)* And so the truth is, I have a hard time getting out of the house. *(Adele hits a button on her phone.)*

ADELE HARTWICK. *(Snapping.)* What is it, Laura?

JENNIFER MARCUS. *(To the audience.)* What I mean is that it's not just OCD anymore. It's maybe, like, kinda, sorta … agoraphobia.

ADELE HARTWICK. *(Angry.)* Slow down! Slow down! I need to get a pen. Jesus!

JENNIFER MARCUS. *(To the audience.)* Though it's not like I'm afraid to leave my house, that's not it. It's just a hell of a lot easier to stay inside where you can manage the germs and the noise and if your dad is on the roof most of the time and you've got some Ethernet cable, it's more like a cathedral than a house. The world, the whole world, you know, can pass right through your house. You don't have to even move. And it's beautiful, you know?

ADELE HARTWICK. Whatever, Laura. You better hope that car

comes or I can't tell you how pissed off I'm gonna be. Keep your cell on. *(Lights down on Adele.)*

JENNIFER MARCUS. *(To the audience.)* I don't blame her for wanting to leave me. I have that effect on people. But she shouldn't have blamed me when I went looking for my real mother. These aren't the lives we were supposed to be living. *(She types something into the computer. To the audience.)* I'm sending you an attachment in two parts, okay? You're going to need these if you want to track Jenny down. *(We hear a "bling" noise from the computer. To the audience.)* The first one is an electronic diary of the days leading up to the Jenny Project. Um, the second part consists of documents, right? They run chronologically with the diary. There are three entries you might want to start with. The first one is dated March fourteenth. I had just gotten fired from my fourth job in five weeks. At the mall it's all about punctuality and nothing about results and anyway, I think owners of the Pretzel Universe and I both agreed it was a case of mutual disdain. *(We hear a doorbell. To the audience.)* So right, March fourteenth. A perfect day to get outside. *(We hear some underscored, excitable music. It should suggest a new beginning, the potential for joy. The clutter in Jennifer's room is removed, the bed makes itself, night turns to day, etc. She removes the silk scarf. Again, a doorbell. Lights up on Adele and Mr. Marcus at the kitchen table. Mr. Marcus is reading the paper, Adele is looking through some work documents. Enter Todd, wearing headphones, manipulating a Rubik's cube and wearing a pizza delivery outfit.)*

TODD. Hello. Hel-lo.

ADELE HARTWICK. *(Loud.)* Jennifer …

TODD. Hel-lo.

ADELE HARTWICK. *(At the documents.)* It's open, Todd. *(Loud.)* Jennifer!

JENNIFER MARCUS. *(Offstage, loud.)* I'm getting ready.

TODD. Fucking-A. *(He rings the doorbell again. Adele gets up, opens the door.)* Hey there.

ADELE HARTWICK. Jennifer's getting ready. *(Adele goes back to the kitchen and her documents.)*

MR. MARCUS. Come on in, Todd.

TODD. Mr. M.

MR. MARCUS. How goes the world of Amechi Pizza, Todd?

TODD. It provides. How goes the world of the newspaper?

MR. MARCUS. It says here these scientists in Belgium think the Neanderthal man was a totally different species.

TODD. Really?

MR. MARCUS. Says the Homo Sapiens either killed him off or wouldn't mate with him.

TODD. I guess it's hard being the ugly guy, Mr. M.

MR. MARCUS. Whatcha got there, a Rubik's cube?

TODD. Yeah. I got two sides a week ago. I don't know though man, this thing is making me nuts. *(Todd puts the cube down on the table.)*

ADELE HARTWICK. What are you doing with yourself these days, Todd?

TODD. Huh? Oh. I'm delivering pizzas.

ADELE HARTWICK. Is that it?

TODD. *(Pause, thinking hard about it.)* Yeah, that's mostly it. *(The music fades. Jennifer enters from the stairs, brushing her hair. She walks a very specific path around the kitchen before she settles in. It should be clear this is a ritual for her and that everyone else is accustomed to it [don't stop the dialogue].)* Wait, I take that back, actually. I'm taking some classes at Pierce College. I'm kinda into this archeology thing.

ADELE HARTWICK. Todd's taking classes, Jennifer, did you hear that?

JENNIFER MARCUS. Yes.

TODD. *(Alien-like, quickly.)* Greetings.

JENNIFER MARCUS. *(Alien-like, quickly.)* Greetings. *(Todd pulls out mail from his apron. Jennifer puts down her brush, picks up the Rubik's cube, starts manipulating it.)*

TODD. Almost forgot. I got the mail for you, Ms. Marcus.

ADELE HARTWICK. That's Jennifer's job, Todd.

TODD. That's some good mail there.

ADELE HARTWICK. It's the only one she can manage to keep these days. You wouldn't want to deprive her. *(Adele starts rifling through the mail.)*

TODD. You got fired again?

JENNIFER MARCUS. I showed up late a lot.

TODD. That's cool.

ADELE HARTWICK. It's not *cool*, Todd.

MR. MARCUS. You helping out Todd with his deliveries today, Jennifer?

JENNIFER MARCUS. Yeah.

MR. MARCUS. Riding co-pilot, eh?

JENNIFER MARCUS. Yeah, Dad.

MR. MARCUS. How's that old Dodge Dart holding up?

TODD. I was thinking of sawing off the roof, going topless.

MR. MARCUS. What if it rains?

TODD. *(Pause.)* Okay, maybe not.

JENNIFER MARCUS. Here. Let's go. *(Jennifer hands Todd back the solved Rubik's cube.)*

TODD. *(In awe.)* Dude. *(Jennifer walks to the door. Opens it with her sleeve. Stands there breathing, trying to make herself cross the threshold.)* How did you do this? I've been working on this for like two months.

JENNIFER MARCUS. It's easy.

MR. MARCUS. You okay there, Jennifer?

JENNIFER MARCUS. I'm okay, Dad.

TODD. You just finished it, right now?

JENNIFER MARCUS. It's really fucking easy, Todd.

TODD. Yeah, well so's walking through a door. *(She is calm, but immobilized in the door frame.)*

ADELE HARTWICK. *(To Jennifer.)* What does the Church of Latter-Day Saints want with you?

JENNIFER MARCUS. What?

ADELE HARTWICK. How do these people get names? *(Adele rips open the seal, reads the letter. Lights dim on Adele, Mr. Marcus and Todd. Lights up on Terrence.)*

TERRENCE. Dear Jennifer. Thank you for spending all this time online with me lately. I don't think I really understand your reading of the Angel Moroni, but I appreciate it. *(She looks up from the door frame.)*

JENNIFER MARCUS. *(To the audience.)* I'd been laying out a litany of inconsistencies found in the Mormon Bible. He's a secular humanist now.

TERRENCE. I wrote to my elders back home and they say I should stop talking to you because they say you're dangerous.

JENNIFER MARCUS. *(To the audience.)* I'd been surfing the net for genealogy sites and I found Terrence in a chat room. These Mormons are fucking obsessed with genealogy!

TERRENCE. And I do think you rely on swears way too much, but I think you're smart and well … don't say this to anyone but I do like it when we talk about sex.

JENNIFER MARCUS. *(To the audience.)* Okay, so I found out he was doing his missionary work in China and in exchange for a little cyberaction …

TERRENCE. So, working off of that certificate of relinquishment you scanned over to me I was able to pull this from some records.

I have a friend who knows some people. Some of it's in Chinese, um, it's your original birth certificate. *(Mr. Marcus puts down his newspaper. Adele looks at the birth certificate.)*

ADELE HARTWICK. What the hell is this?

TERRENCE. You were born in a tiny village called Maigon-ko. Your real mother's name is Su Yang Chow. Or Chow Su Yang. It's last name first over here. Um, there's no father recorded. Sorry. You can't tell anyone where you got this. And don't tell anyone about our chats, okay? See you online. Your brother in the celestial kingdom, Terrence. *(Lights down on Terrence. Jennifer runs from the door and grabs the letter and birth certificate from Adele.)*

JENNIFER MARCUS. That's mine.

ADELE HARTWICK. What the hell is this?

MR. MARCUS. I knew a Mormon once. He had a great wink.

JENNIFER MARCUS. I'm sorry, Todd. I don't think I can go today. I can't get out the door.

TODD. Huh?

ADELE HARTWICK. What have you been up to, young lady?

JENNIFER MARCUS. None of your goddamn business.

ADELE HARTWICK. What have you done, Jennifer?

TODD. I'm think I'm gonna go now. *(Todd exits.)*

JENNIFER MARCUS. *(To Adele.)* You shouldn't be opening my fucking mail. *(Jennifer runs up to her room. Adele looks back at Mr. Marcus.)*

MR. MARCUS. He had this wink. Made you feel warm inside. *(Lights down on Mr. Marcus and Adele. Jennifer reads the note.)*

JENNIFER MARCUS. Wow. Six pounds, five ounces. A girl. Chow Su Yang. Chow — Su — Yang. My mother. *(She takes a breath then looks up. To the audience.)* The only thing that saved me, saved the whole house from total chaos was a small decorating company in some place called Duluth, Minnesota. A potential acquisition or some utterly fucking boring thing that was up with Mom's company. A place where it's cold but not cold enough to freeze your cell phone. It's March twentieth. There should be a phone record with it. Check that shit out. She calls the house fourteen times that day. The day I make contact with China again. *(Lights up on Todd at the front door. He is holding a pizza box.)*

TODD. *(Alien-like.)* Greetings, gestures.

JENNIFER MARCUS. *(Alien-like.)* Greetings received. *(She takes the pizza and finishes the final leg of her usual path through the kitchen. Todd follows right behind her as they talk.)* Hey. Sorry about finishing your Rubik's cube.

TODD. No, that's cool. I've had some time to reflect and I think I overreacted. I just hate feeling dumb.

JENNIFER MARCUS. You're not dumb. The Rubik's cube only works a certain part of the brain.

TODD. Yeah, well, that must be the part of the brain that's writing my mid-terms.

JENNIFER MARCUS. What did you get?

TODD. All C's. I got a C-plus in archeology! I fucking love that class! The professor's taking the A students on a dig to Peru or somewhere to look for artifacts and bones and I don't know, it's gonna be totally cool and I'm not gonna get to go.

JENNIFER MARCUS. I could write your papers for you. *(Mr. Marcus enters.)*

TODD. That's not the point now, is it?

MR. MARCUS. What did Mr. Amechi bring us today?

TODD. Hey, Mr. M.

MR. MARCUS. Anchovies and pineapple! Fish-a-liscious, cow-abunga! *(He waits for a reaction, Jennifer and Todd stare at him. We hear the phone ring.)* I wonder who that is?

JENNIFER MARCUS. I'm not here.

MR. MARCUS. Do you mind if I …

JENNIFER MARCUS. Take it, Dad.

MR. MARCUS. Hello? Hey, you. How's Duluth? *(He takes a slice of pizza offstage, listening to Adele on the phone.)*

TODD. Where's your mom?

JENNIFER MARCUS. Out of town, thank God.

TODD. So what was that scene all about last week? Your mom was totally ass.

JENNIFER MARCUS. Yeah, I know.

TODD. What's up?

JENNIFER MARCUS. I've been trying to find my biological mother.

TODD. Dude.

JENNIFER MARCUS. Some guy I met online's been doing some research for me.

TODD. Heavy.

JENNIFER MARCUS. Yeah, Lady Hartwick did not approve.

TODD. I've got four words for you. Proceed — with — caution.

JENNIFER MARCUS. I was just curious.

TODD. Yeah, but I know you. Once you start something it's like no longer a conversation.

JENNIFER MARCUS. I know what I'm doing.

TODD. I know you're mom's a raging pain and all, but it's not all bad, ya know. I mean, c'mon, you got Tivo.

JENNIFER MARCUS. I got a right to know, ya know.

TODD. It's a thing, that's all I'm saying. You start making it mom versus mom. It gets ugly. You might want to think about bringing that into the house.

JENNIFER MARCUS. Noted.

TODD. End of lecture. I got a Bell Canyon delivery in the car. Gotta ride.

JENNIFER MARCUS. Todd, what do you want for your birthday?

TODD. Oh, yeah. I'm getting old. Well, the Mexican guy at work, Carlos, he's got these beaded seat cushions.

JENNIFER MARCUS. I'll see what I can do. *(She hands him a twenty.)* Keep the change.

TODD. I will. I will keep this change. I will make this change mine. I will love this change like it was my brother. I will surround it with light and take it to the holy man … *(Todd exits.)*

MR. MARCUS. *(Into the phone.)* So what's an RFP, again? *(Jennifer closes the front door with her sleeve and goes to the kitchen, grabs a slice of pizza.)* I have too been listening. She's right here. *(Jennifer shakes her head.)* It's your mother. *(She rolls her eyes, takes the slice with her to her room. Into the phone.)* She's gonna take it upstairs. When are you coming home? Well, when do you think? *(Jennifer goes to her computer, types something.)* They got a new fire truck down at the station, Carl said I could ride with the boys this weekend. *(Jennifer picks up the phone.)*

JENNIFER MARCUS. *(Into the phone.)* And for the hundredth time today … *(Lights up on Adele.)*

ADELE HARTWICK. I just got off the phone with your father and we've decided a few things.

JENNIFER MARCUS. Let me guess …

JENNIFER MARCUS and ADELE HARTWICK. There's going to be some changes.

MR. MARCUS. I'll just let you two girls gab, how'sthatokaygood … *(Mr. Marcus hangs up, exits with the pizza and the phone.)*

JENNIFER MARCUS. You're just pissed off 'cause of the letter.

ADELE HARTWICK. Actually I'm going to pretend that never happened.

JENNIFER MARCUS. Why? 'Cause you embarrassed yourself?

ADELE HARTWICK. Me? I'm not the cybersex addict.

JENNIFER MARCUS. *(Laughing.)* Cybersex addict!

ADELE HARTWICK. I don't have time for your crap, Jennifer.

JENNIFER MARCUS. *(Laughing.)* Whatever!

ADELE HARTWICK. If you want to go find out who your mother is, go ahead. I'm not going to stop you. But it's not, and I repeat, it is not going to be a full-time job. *(Jennifer begins typing into her computer.)*

JENNIFER MARCUS. Whatever you say, Mom.

ADELE HARTWICK. You are going to help your father out around the house. You are going to go outside and that does not mean car rides with Todd.

JENNIFER MARCUS. Okay, Mom.

ADELE HARTWICK. You are going to open the paper every day and look for another job. You are going to go on interviews. You are going to go back into therapy and you are going to recommit yourself to functioning in the *real* world.

JENNIFER MARCUS. Okay.

ADELE HARTWICK. And after that, if there's time, you can spend the rest of your life tracking down that woman who abandoned you. Okay, Jennifer?

JENNIFER MARCUS. Okay, *Adele.*

ADELE HARTWICK. *(Pause, steamed.)* Give me your father.

JENNIFER MARCUS. *(Loud.)* Dad! *(We hear a "boink" noise from the computer. Jennifer's eyes open wide.)* Terrence!

ADELE HARTWICK. Are you online?!

JENNIFER MARCUS. Dad!

MR. MARCUS. *(Offstage.)* I got it. *(Jennifer hangs up the phone.)*

ADELE HARTWICK. Jennifer!

MR. MARCUS. *(Offstage.)* It's me.

ADELE HARTWICK. *(Frustrated.)* I'll be home Friday, Mark. *(Lights out on Adele. Lights up on Terrence, typing at a computer in a Taco Bell in Shanghai, China. We hear people talking in Chinese. Interspersed, we hear words like "Mexi-melt" and "chimichanga.")*

JENNIFER MARCUS. *(Typing back.)* Terrence! I'm here. Hey! How's your mission going?

TERRENCE. Not so great, actually. I'm not myself. I keep thinking about that stuff you told me about the geology.

JENNIFER MARCUS. The archeological record just doesn't back up the Mormon account of early North America. Sorry, Terrence.

TERRENCE. Yeah, well, it's really hard trying to convert some-

24

one when you've got that in your head. My companion, Obadiah, thinks I'm worthless.

JENNIFER MARCUS. Hey, where are you?

TERRENCE. I'm in Shanghai. *(Beat.)* At a Taco Bell.

JENNIFER MARCUS. They've got Taco Bells in Shanghai?

TERRENCE. Well, I don't think these are the same beans they use in Provo but they've got Internet connections in the booths.

JENNIFER MARCUS. That's kind of cool.

TERRENCE. I got your email. I'm glad you got the birth certificate, it took some work.

JENNIFER MARCUS. Yeah, thanks again. But could you not send stuff by regular mail anymore, okay? I'm having some privacy issues here at the house and well, let's just do things by email and instant message, okay?

TERRENCE. Okay!

JENNIFER MARCUS. Great! So hey, look, could you do me another favor?

TERRENCE. Okay!

JENNIFER MARCUS. I need you to keep looking for her. Su Yang.

TERRENCE. Do you know how many Chows there are in China?

JENNIFER MARCUS. How's your ejaculation problem going?

TERRENCE. *(Looks around, panicked.)* Jennifer!

JENNIFER MARCUS. What?

TERRENCE. I'm at a Taco Bell!

JENNIFER MARCUS. So?

TERRENCE. *(Nervous.)* Oh gosh. Jeez. Um, jeez. I'm up to about 80 seconds.

JENNIFER MARCUS. Well, that's still not long enough. No girl is ever gonna stand for that, Terrence.

TERRENCE. It's hard!

JENNIFER MARCUS. What are you doing when you do it?

TERRENCE. Jennifer!

JENNIFER MARCUS. Terrence, I need to know where Su Yang lives. You don't think you can do it?

TERRENCE. No. I can find her. Um … uh … Can you send me another picture?

JENNIFER MARCUS. Tits or ass?

TERRENCE. Uhhh …

JENNIFER MARCUS. Jesus, hold on. *(Jennifer pulls her pants down, points her butt at the computer camera and reaches back with her hand.)* How's this? *(She hits one button on the computer. We hear a "bling" noise from the computer. Terrence looks at his screen then immediately covers it.)*

TERRENCE. Oh God. *(Jennifer pulls up her pants, goes back to typing.)*

JENNIFER MARCUS. You'll look for her?

TERRENCE. Yeah, yeah. *(He prematurely ejaculates right there at Taco Bell.)*

JENNIFER MARCUS. Next time we talk I want to hear you made it five minutes. Do you hear me, boy?

TERRENCE. Yes, ma'am.

JENNIFER MARCUS. Good. And don't yank so hard.

TERRENCE. Okay.

JENNIFER MARCUS. Find me. *(Lights down on Terrence. To the audience.)* Don't start getting any pervy ideas about nudie pics, okay? Terrence, I can trust. You? You probably got like, clumps of old-person-hair on your back. You stick to the diary, okay? *(We hear a "blip" noise from the computer. To the audience.)* Friday, March twenty-eighth. My mother is being driven back from the airport with a glass of whateversinthecar, straight up. *(We hear gentle, quieting music. A lullaby for an asteroid field. To the audience.)* There's a meteor shower that night. Remnants of the asteroid U-152 are speeding to their death. It's pretty cool. Me? *(Lights up on Mr. Marcus, looking through his binoculars. To the audience.)* I'm sharing a blanket with my father, up on the balcony. *(She pulls out a small tool kit and a prototype cube and gets under the blanket.)*

MR. MARCUS. Ooh, there's one. *(Pause.)* There's another one. *(Pause.)* Oooh, that one had a green tail. Did you see that one?

JENNIFER MARCUS. No. *(He puts down the binoculars.)*

MR. MARCUS. Whatcha working on there, kiddo?

JENNIFER MARCUS. Oh, nothing. Just, whatever. Something for Todd.

MR. MARCUS. Is that right?

JENNIFER MARCUS. I'm trying to make a replacement for his Rubik's cube. I think, ya know, he was kind of mad at me.

MR. MARCUS. I like that guy, Todd. He's a *cool* guy.

JENNIFER MARCUS. Me too.

MR. MARCUS. Do you *like him* like him?

JENNIFER MARCUS. We're just friends, Dad.

MR. MARCUS. Oh. *(Pause, yawns.)* I wonder where your mom is? Oh boy, there goes another one!

JENNIFER MARCUS. Todd used to like me like that. When I was the mascot.

MR. MARCUS. The conquistador. Yeah, that was fun watching you. Cheering the team. I remember how nervous I got when you went to the top of the pyramid.

JENNIFER MARCUS. It's no biggie.

MR. MARCUS. Yeah, I used to say, that's my girl up there. Then you'd leap off, doing those splits ... *(Picks up the binoculars again.)* Look at that big sucker! *(Puts the binoculars back down.)* Don't you like meteors?

JENNIFER MARCUS. Just a bunch of rocks burning up into nothing.

MR. MARCUS. *(Nudging her.)* Someone must have given them bum directions, eh?

JENNIFER MARCUS. Yeah, Dad. *(Mr. Marcus yawns. Jennifer stops working on her present for Todd.)* Why doesn't she like me?

MR. MARCUS. Who?

JENNIFER MARCUS. Mom.

MR. MARCUS. Why do you say that? Your mother loves you.

JENNIFER MARCUS. Why is she always such a hard-ass?

MR. MARCUS. Now, you shouldn't say that ...

JENNIFER MARCUS. You know what I mean. *(They sit there for a moment.)*

MR. MARCUS. When I got injured, we didn't have anything saved up. My settlement was fair, but nothing we could live off of. And it took a while to kick in. Your mother had to work three jobs to keep us going. Woke up, made me breakfast. Went to work. Came home. Drove me to therapy. Went back to work. Picked me up. Made me dinner. Two years of that.

JENNIFER MARCUS. Yeah.

MR. MARCUS. Do you know when we went to China? And they put you in her arms. Do you know what she said? Do you?

JENNIFER MARCUS. No.

MR. MARCUS. She said to the people at the adoption house, she looks up at them and says, "You knew." She looked at me and said "They knew. They knew, Mark. Look at her. She's perfect. They picked the perfect girl for us." And she cried. Cried a lot. She was so happy.

JENNIFER MARCUS. Really?

MR. MARCUS. Let me tell you something, kiddo. I think parents ... I think parents are hardest on the kids that are most like them-

27

selves. *(He yawns again. Adele enters, sits down in the kitchen, in the dark.)* Wow, that was another big one.

JENNIFER MARCUS. But I'm nothing like her.

MR. MARCUS. Oh, I don't know about that. You're both smart.

JENNIFER MARCUS. I'm smarter.

MR. MARCUS. You're both a little arrogant.

JENNIFER MARCUS. I didn't ...

MR. MARCUS. Shush. You're both stubborn. Fiercely independent. *(He closes his eyes.)* And I think your mom was a little hurt. *(Yawns.)* When you didn't tell her what you were up to.

JENNIFER MARCUS. I'm not up to anything. I was just curious.

MR. MARCUS. I know. It's natural.

JENNIFER MARCUS. I just want to know who she is. You're my parents, this isn't some dumb-ass identity thing. It's just sometimes ... I don't, ya know. I'm tired of her ragging on me all the time. I'm trying, ya know. *(Pause.)* I'm having a hard time lately. *(Pause.)* Wow. That one almost hit the ground. Did you see that, Dad? *(Jennifer looks over at Mr. Marcus. He is asleep. She puts her part of the blanket over him. The music fades. She picks up her cube and tool kit and walks to the kitchen where Adele is sitting, waiting, staring off into space, with a drink in her hand [she's plowed].)* Oh.

ADELE HARTWICK. Hi.

JENNIFER MARCUS. How was your trip?

ADELE HARTWICK. It was what it was.

JENNIFER MARCUS. How was the acquisition?

ADELE HARTWICK. It happened. How come the garbage is still in the back, Jennifer?

JENNIFER MARCUS. I forgot.

ADELE HARTWICK. What are we going to do with you, Jennifer?

JENNIFER MARCUS. Welcome back, Mom. *(Jennifer turns to leave.)*

ADELE HARTWICK. No. We're not finished.

JENNIFER MARCUS. I'm tired.

ADELE HARTWICK. You're tired? No, you're not. You haven't been in fourteen-hour negotiations. Your secretary didn't forget to book you a room. You weren't rerouted three times this week. You didn't have to fire a lifetime employee, someone who's been with the company for twenty-eight years and barely makes enough to support his family. And you sure as hell didn't do it the same day the company picked up a two-thousand-dollar-dinner. You're not tired, Jennifer. I'm tired.

JENNIFER MARCUS. Okay. Then you should probably go to bed.

ADELE HARTWICK. No. I can't go to bed because my house is in disarray.

JENNIFER MARCUS. What are you talking about?

ADELE HARTWICK. Take out the garbage. Do some dishes. Am I asking too much?

JENNIFER MARCUS. I've been busy.

ADELE HARTWICK. Online. With your little cyber-boyfriend …

JENNIFER MARCUS. You're drunk.

ADELE HARTWICK. … Hello cyberfriend. Can you find my mommy for me?

JENNIFER MARCUS. Whatever.

ADELE HARTWICK. You think you're a princess …

JENNIFER MARCUS. You're totally plowed.

ADELE HARTWICK. … A little Chinese princess? Isn't that what you think? Think your father and I stole you away from the queen? We're keeping you from your life as the emperor's daughter, huh?

JENNIFER MARCUS. Shut up.

ADELE HARTWICK. What happened to you, Jennifer?

JENNIFER MARCUS. You happened to me.

ADELE HARTWICK. Oh, is that right? I ruined your life? Me, who got on a plane, brought you back here. Put you in this house, put you into every accelerated program, every activity. Fed your brain.

JENNIFER MARCUS. I didn't ask for this house and I hated those classes.

ADELE HARTWICK. *(Reliving it.)* Ms. Hartwick, Mr. Marcus. Your little girl's a genius. What do you do, Jennifer?

JENNIFER MARCUS. I don't care.

ADELE HARTWICK. You can't even imagine. Of course you can't, you weren't there. You were out on the playground. They give you a handbook.

JENNIFER MARCUS. Oh, of course, the handbook …

ADELE HARTWICK. Page one. Never tell them they're a genius.

JENNIFER MARCUS. Never tell them you're good at anything …

ADELE HARTWICK. Page two …

JENNIFER MARCUS. How to deprive your child of joy and wonder while preparing her for a life of infinite servitude.

ADELE HARTWICK. She abandoned you.

JENNIFER MARCUS. Yeah? Then how come her name is on the birth certificate? *(The following dialogue overlaps until "GO!")*

ADELE HARTWICK. … left you on a doorstep …

JENNIFER MARCUS. How would they know that?

ADELE HARTWICK. … and you want to *replace* me?

JENNIFER MARCUS. This isn't about the fucking garbage cans.

ADELE HARTWICK. You don't know what we've done for you.

JENNIFER MARCUS. It's maybe I'll like her more. Isn't that it?

ADELE HARTWICK. You had so much potential …

JENNIFER MARCUS. She loved me.

ADELE HARTWICK. A brilliant child. And I am …

JENNIFER MARCUS. And I'm going to find her.

ADELE HARTWICK. … totally mystified by what has happened to you.

JENNIFER MARCUS. Did you hear me? I'm getting the fuck out of here.

ADELE HARTWICK. Go. GO! *(Jennifer heads for the front door.)*

JENNIFER MARCUS. I'm going to find her. I want to meet my real mother.

ADELE HARTWICK. Yeah, and how are you going to do that?

JENNIFER MARCUS. I'll fly.

ADELE HARTWICK. You got a passport?

JENNIFER MARCUS. I'll get one.

ADELE HARTWICK. You have a travel visa?

JENNIFER MARCUS. I'll contact the Embassy. *(Jennifer opens the front door.)*

ADELE HARTWICK. Yeah? And how are you going to get to the airport, huh? How are you going to get out the front door? *(Jennifer stands in the door frame. She is breathing hard.)* They make names up, Jennifer. They do that, you know? They just fill in the blank. And that's the truth. There's probably a thousand birth certificates with her name on it. And that silly scarf you wear around … probably the nurse's. The truth? That woman abandoned you. And your father and I took two years filling out paperwork, getting signatures and mortgaging our lives into the stratosphere so we could get on a plane, to a scary country where we knew *no one!* So we could save your life. *(Jennifer keeps putting one foot out the door and then bringing it back in.)* We would never give up on you. We love you. And that is why I push you. That is why I won't let you accept this as your life. And I'll be damned if I'm going to let you throw it away, let you spend it with flunkies like Todd, people with

30

not an *ounce* of ambition. *(Jennifer is trying not to lose it in front of Adele, who slowly walks towards her.)* Listen to me. Listen. My daughter is brilliant. My daughter is an exceptional young woman. And I am not going to let her waste away. *(Adele tries to hug Jennifer from behind.)*

JENNIFER MARCUS. *(Freaking out.)* Don't you touch me! Don't you ever fucking touch me again! *(She runs away from Adele, back to the kitchen, shaking out her hands frantically.)*

ADELE HARTWICK. I live in the real world, Jennifer. I'm real. And in the real world, women get screwed out there and if you're not prepared they will squash you. So blame me, lash out at me for your condition, but don't …

JENNIFER MARCUS. I'm going to find her. I'm going to China.

ADELE HARTWICK. Sure, go to China when you can't even take out the garbage. Keep dreaming.

JENNIFER MARCUS. I'm going there. You watch me. *(She runs to her room, past Mr. Marcus. Adele shuts the front door.)*

MR. MARCUS. What the hell is going on down here?

ADELE HARTWICK. *(Loud.)* The only way you're going to get to China is if this house grows wings.

MR. MARCUS. Adele … *(Adele exits, followed by Mr. Marcus. Jennifer sits down at her computer, typing feverishly.)*

ADELE HARTWICK. *(Offstage, loud.)* I'm real. This house is real, Jennifer. And you can hide in your room and log on if you want to. But that's not real! That's a dream! *(We hear a door slam.)*

JENNIFER MARCUS. Dear Dr. Yakunin. It's me, Jennifer Marcus. I know you haven't heard from me in a while, but I need to talk to you immediately. You're the only person I know who'll understand. Find me, please. I need your help. *(She stops typing.)* I'm going to build a robot. *(She hits a button on her computer and we hear a "bling" noise. Blackout. We hear the music from the play's opening. Lights up on Dr. Yakunin. He is at his computer, talking directly to a tiny camera attached to the monitor.)*

DR. YAKUNIN. Jennifer Marcus … Jennifer Marcus … what is this face to me? I am confused. I am thinking in my head — who sends email out of cloud? Who sends this flare fired over wintry field, lighting up the world, lighting up everything? Jennifer Marcus you say? Hmmmm. Okay give me second for me to shake … "dusty cobwebs" from time machine in brain. Hmmmmmm. Wait, I knew a Marcus! But this cannot be same girl. No. No. The little genius from California? This shooting star who starts revolution in cognitive artificial intelligence at give me break, high school science fair?! Go screw me with spirit stick, I cannot believe you! *(Lights up on Jennifer at her computer, trying to be as patient as she is capable of. Music begins to fade out.)* This is the Jennifer Marcus who I write fourteen letters of recommendation to universities for?! This same girl who takes letters and flushes them down Johnny toilet seat?!

JENNIFER MARCUS. *(To the audience.)* Okay, so I had like forgotten what is was like to teleconference with Dr. Yakunin.

DR. YAKUNIN. The Jennifer Marcus that left me for dead man? She takes my dreams for her, no she takes my heart, that's what she does, rips it out of my chest! She shows it to my face, takes pulsing heart, shoves it in horse's ass, horse trots into street, horse gets hit by truck, truck explodes, gasoline back in my face, FACE BURN, flesh fall off of face! Dr. Yakunin no longer allowed in fancy restaurant. What happened to you? Some little genius girl, some girl you decide to mentor, take under your special wing — Hmmmm? She take a big shit on you? Leave hot, steamy log on your back? No, you scare away customers! OUT! BACK AWAY! Away into stupid world of rotting flesh. NOOOO!

JENNIFER MARCUS. *(To the audience.)* He sure does talk a lot and I forgot, he's got this like, Shakespearean sense of betrayal.

DR. YAKUNIN. This Jennifer Marcus, no, she was just glimpse. A fiery gem. A little glimmer of cosmic luminescence. She entered like a god and when she left, we had no god. Who are you?

JENNIFER MARCUS. It's me, Dr. Yakunin.

DR. YAKUNIN. *(Pause.)* Yes. So it is. *(Clears his throat.)* So you want to get back in the robotics game, do you? Yes, this is intriguing. I tell you same thing I tell Ms. Yakunin when she wants to trim my nose hair. *(Yells.)* DON'T FUCKING DO IT!

JENNIFER MARCUS. *(To the audience.)* Dr. Yakunin ...

DR. YAKUNIN. And I am very busy right now, Jennifer. Very bad time. Busy. Busy. I have the preparing for the conference, the eleventh annual stupid International Workshop on Human and Machine Cognition. I don't know why, the first ten were a farce!

JENNIFER MARCUS. *(To the audience.)* It's very hard to keep his attention sometimes.

DR. YAKUNIN. Free exchange of ideas. Some fucking ideas! Roschenmeyer, he still can't take seriously, general notion of android point of view. I sit in my chair, I do this whole time. *(He picks up a telephone book and starts smashing his face with it.)*

JENNIFER MARCUS. *(To the audience.)* There is, of course, one way to get through to him. *(To the computer.)* Dr. Yakunin?

DR. YAKUNIN. WHAT???!!!

JENNIFER MARCUS. I read your article. The new one in the *Atlantic Journal of Science*. The one on revising the standard automata hierarchy. I thought it was totally cool.

DR. YAKUNIN. That little thing? Well, hmmm. It was nothing.

JENNIFER MARCUS. Long overdue if you ask me.

DR. YAKUNIN. WELL, YES, OF COURSE! The current model is a fossil, anyone could see that! If they bother to revisit!

JENNIFER MARCUS. How come you're not at MIT anymore?

DR. YAKUNIN. FUCK THOSE FACISTS! They cut off funds. They say, android epistemology? No one dreams in macro anymore, just little piss-ant projects.

JENNIFER MARCUS. Where are you now? *(Dr. Yakunin gets a pained expression on his face.)* Dr. Yakunin?

DR. YAKUNIN. Don't want to talk about it.

JENNIFER MARCUS. Cornell? Harvard?

DR. YAKUNIN. I'm in ... *New Haven.*

JENNIFER MARCUS. Yale?

DR. YAKUNIN. DON'T WANT TO TALK!

JENNIFER MARCUS. I'm so sorry.

DR. YAKUNIN. It's a shambles, Jennifer! They say, look here, here's your computer lab. I say why don't you throw some straw on the floor and get SOME GOATS IN HERE! IT'S A FUCKING DISGRACE!

JENNIFER MARCUS. You deserve better.

DR. YAKUNIN. I got a whole studio of rejects. I tell them first day, you should all be RIVERBOAT CAPTAINS. I say you, why do you want to pursue robotics. Oh, I don't know. You, you with the unfortunate haircut. I read your term paper from last year. You tell me robot can be both simultaneously intelligent and infallible. GET OUT OF MY FUCKING CLASSROOM!

JENNIFER MARCUS. Dr. Yakunin?

DR. YAKUNIN. WHAT CHILD?!

JENNIFER MARCUS. Are you going to help me?

DR. YAKUNIN. Why do you have to do this?

JENNIFER MARCUS. I guess I miss it, ya know?

DR. YAKUNIN. Bullshit.

JENNIFER MARCUS. No really, I've been like, laying around thinking ...

DR. YAKUNIN. Sounds exciting, Jennifer. I have enough wishy-washy students. I am very busy. I have to go … *(She hits herself in the head.)*

JENNIFER MARCUS. Three weeks ago I found out who my biological mother is and that she might be living in China. I want to meet her except I have this condition and it like won't let me go out of my house. Okay, so, I'm afraid to leave my house, alright. So, I guess I thought, if I could figure out how to build a propulsion system requiring a basic but stable energy source and attach it to an android simulation of myself, one that would be capable of self-navigation, conceptual thinking and language comprehension, that I could in a sorta-kinda way, go and be with my mother. *(He thinks about it for a moment.)*

DR. YAKUNIN. That's pretty good reason. *(Pause.)* Okay, I help you. What can I do?

JENNIFER MARCUS. Well, um, um, I need parts. Appendages.

DR. YAKUNIN. How much money you have?

JENNIFER MARCUS. I have about two hundred sixteen dollars in my bank account.

DR. YAKUNIN. THAT'S NOT GOING TO DO IT!

JENNIFER MARCUS. I know.

DR. YAKUNIN. I'll tell you what. I know some people. *(Clears throat.)* You have any ethical problems working on missiles?

JENNIFER MARCUS. Should I?

DR. YAKUNIN. Don't ask me that!

JENNIFER MARCUS. Okay, no.

DR. YAKUNIN. Good answer.

JENNIFER MARCUS. Cool.

DR. YAKUNIN. It's going to be boring for you.

JENNIFER MARCUS. Whatever, I don't care.

DR. YAKUNIN. You got a lab? You got tools?

JENNIFER MARCUS. Some.

DR. YAKUNIN. Alright, I send you stuff. You set up the fake business name, all that shit. You get call in few days. You have to negotiate hard! These people are idiots but they count every light bulb. Now parts, yes, I think there's a robotic arm here. I saw one in the JANITOR'S CLOSET! FUCKING NEW HAVEN! A fucking barn, I tell you!

JENNIFER MARCUS. Thank you sooo much.

DR. YAKUNIN. I get you easy job, you do it quick and spend rest of time working on android. I send you notes for lecture, details on instinctual programming. You send me progress report always. Hopefully, in time for conference in July where we show the cowards again, what we can do! Agreed?!

JENNIFER MARCUS. Totally agreed.

DR. YAKUNIN. The little genius! *(Clears throat.)* You look like shit. Take a shower. *(Lights down on Dr. Yakunin.)*

JENNIFER MARCUS. *(To the audience.)* Okay, I'm sending you the second half of my diary. This will cover the days and nights of what we're calling the Jenny Project. *(We hear a "bling" noise from the computer. To the audience.)* The first entry is April second. *(We hear a phone ring. To the audience.)* A phone call from Bethesda, Maryland. My mother, who was feeling pretty weak about the fight we had, and I guess so was I, well you know, she decided to like work from home. Anyway, she answered the phone. *(The phone rings again. Adele enters and answers it.)*

ADELE HARTWICK. Hello? Who? *Who* is this? *Alright.* Hold on just a second. *(She covers the receiver with one hand. Loud.)* Jennifer!

JENNIFER MARCUS. *(Loud.)* I got it. *(Jennifer picks up the phone.)*

ADELE HARTWICK. It's the Army.

JENNIFER MARCUS. *(Mouthing "oh fuck" then:)* Okay, I got it.

ADELE HARTWICK. I'm not even going to ask. *(Adele clicks off the phone, and exits. Lights up on Colonel Patrick Hubbard.)*

COL. HUBBARD. Is this Hartwick Intelligent Logistics?

JENNIFER MARCUS. *(Very nervous.)* Huh? Oh, yeah.

COL. HUBBARD. I'm trying to reach the CEO, a Ms. Jennifer Marcus?

JENNIFER MARCUS. That's me. Uh, sorry about that. That was our temp. She's older and well, not used to working in our industry.

COL. HUBBARD. I see, well, good afternoon, Ms. Marcus. My name is Colonel Patrick Hubbard, and I'm not calling from the Army per se, I'm at the Department of Defense. I got your name from Dr. Michael Yakunin. He said your company might be interested in some work. Your people come highly recommended.

JENNIFER MARCUS. Uh, yeah, right. I'm listening. *(She tries to occupy herself to stay calm. Bouncing on the bed, cleaning the blinds, etc.)*

COL. HUBBARD. Good, then. Let me spell out the situation we're at here. The current administration has done an about-face on the surface-to-air budget. It's put a turtle in our pants, so to speak, Ms. Marcus.

JENNIFER MARCUS. Oh, uh, call me Jennifer.

COL. HUBBARD. Okay, Jennifer, thing is, we're gonna have to

lean heavily on some of our older stockpiles. Now, there's just one problem with that. They're old. Got parts that need replacing. And well, we no longer have these parts. And to be perfectly honest, we no longer know how to build them. Some drunk-ass sergeant went and shredded the wrong documents. Just another Friday around here, get me. This is where your company …

JENNIFER MARCUS. Hartwick Intelligent Logistics.

COL. HUBBARD. Yes, this is where you come in. We need you to reengineer some guidance systems and have them adapt to our current technology.

JENNIFER MARCUS. You mean your missiles can't talk with your satellites.

COL. HUBBARD. That's the skinny of it, yes, ma'am.

JENNIFER MARCUS. Well, that's a fucking no-brainer.

COL. HUBBARD. Ma'am? *(She quickly puts the phone down, bangs her head into the bookcase.)*

JENNIFER MARCUS. Stupid. *(Back into the phone.)* I mean that sounds like a problem. But, nothing we can't handle.

COL. HUBBARD. Well, good then. Hell, that's terrific. Dr. Yakunin tells me you and your team practically work out of your garage and frankly that kind of quirkiness suits us just fine. See these missiles they're like our eighth line of defense and well the administration hasn't exactly filled our donkeys with cream cheese, if you know what I mean.

JENNIFER MARCUS. Not exactly.

COL. HUBBARD. We don't have a lot of money.

JENNIFER MARCUS. Well, Colonel Hubbard …

COL. HUBBARD. Call me Patrick.

JENNIFER MARCUS. Cool, Patrick. Cool. Um, yeah, well, I think we can work something out. Of course, we're in the middle of a robotics project for a Korean company. *(She slaps her face.)* Uh, that's South Korea, of course.

COL. HUBBARD. I should hope.

JENNIFER MARCUS. *(Crossing her fingers.)* Anyway, like, maybe we can work out a trade. We fix your parts, you provide some to … us?

COL. HUBBARD. Well, Jennifer, the Department of Defense has some policies when it comes to bartering, but if you don't mind working through a subcontractor at Raytheon, I think, how do those Koreans say it, I think we've got good kimchi.

JENNIFER MARCUS. *(Jumping on the bed.)* Ha. Good one.

COL. HUBBARD. Great. Your contact's name at Raytheon is a

man named Preston. He'll send you the work and set you up with everything you need.

JENNIFER MARCUS. *(Pushing it, quickly.)* We're also gonna need schematics on your satellites and access into your networks ...

COL. HUBBARD. Just talk to Preston, he'll set it up.

JENNIFER MARCUS. Awesome.

COL. HUBBARD. *(Shaking his head.)* Californians. Nice talking to you, Jennifer. The Department of Defense welcomes you to its family. *(Lights out on Hubbard.)*

JENNIFER MARCUS. Alright. Thanks. *(She hangs up, falls back into the bed, screaming into her pillow, kicking her feet up and down. We hear some excitable underscoring.)* Ahhhhhh yeah! *(She dances her "dance of great joy." We hear a doorbell.)*

ADELE HARTWICK. *(Offstage.)* Jennifer! *(Jennifer runs to her window, looks out.)*

JENNIFER MARCUS. Oh boy. Okay. Okay. *(She picks up something off her desk, puts it in her pocket.)*

ADELE HARTWICK. *(Offstage.)* You have a visitor, Jennifer.

JENNIFER MARCUS. I'm coming. *(She runs downstairs. We hear the doorbell again. Muttering.)* Keep it together, Marcus. You can do this. Red leader, this is gold leader, stay on target, *(Explosion noise.)* stay on target ... *(She follows about half the same intricate path in the kitchen she usually does, then says ...)* Fuck it. *(Lights up on Todd at the front door with a pizza.)*

TODD. *(Monotoned.)* Greetings and salutations.

JENNIFER MARCUS. Hey. *(He gives her the pizza.)* Can you break a fifty?

TODD. Ummm ...

JENNIFER MARCUS. I'm just kidding. I want you to keep it.

TODD. Huh?

JENNIFER MARCUS. I need you to open a P.O. box for me.

TODD. Why? You buy some sexy toys or something? *(Mr. Marcus enters, music fades out.)*

MR. MARCUS. Hey, Todd.

TODD. Hey, Mr. M.

MR. MARCUS. What's on the pizza?

JENNIFER MARCUS. Same as always.

MR. MARCUS. Fish-a-licious ...

TODD. Cowabunga.

MR. MARCUS. Cowabunga. That's right. *(He looks out the door.)* Say, you really did saw off that roof, didn't ya?

TODD. Best driving I've ever had, Mr. M. The chicks really dig it.

MR. MARCUS. Well that's fine. Let's just make sure this little chick doesn't dig it.

JENNIFER MARCUS. Dad!

MR. MARCUS. I'm just kidding, I know you two use protection.

JENNIFER MARCUS. *(Totally embarrassed.)* Jesus Christ!

MR. MARCUS. Of course Todd, the roof is what holds the car together, the whole thing's probably going to cave in on you now. You crazy kid. Give me a high-five!

TODD. Huh?

MR. MARCUS. C'mon! It'll be fun.

TODD. Okay. *(Todd gives him a cautious high five.)*

MR. MARCUS. See? *(He exits with the pizza.)*

TODD. Is he right about my car?

JENNIFER MARCUS. Todd, forget it! Listen. I'm going to be getting a lot of packages in the mail. And I'm going to need you to like, pick them up and bring them to me.

TODD. What kind of packages?

JENNIFER MARCUS. Magical packages. WHAT THE FUCK?!

TODD. Alright! Keep it in your pants! I don't need to know. I'll do it.

JENNIFER MARCUS. You got a pen?

TODD. Yeah, here. *(She starts writing on his hand.)*

JENNIFER MARCUS. You need to set up the mailbox under this name.

TODD. What's going on?

JENNIFER MARCUS. I'll tell you about it later.

TODD. Okay. Whatever. But, I'm telling you. You should be working on getting out of the house. You should come do some deliveries with me. We'll listen to some Rush … *(She gives him the pen, then starts wiping her hands on her sides, then shaking her hands out again.)*

JENNIFER MARCUS. I can't.

TODD. *(Reading his hand.)* Hartwick Intelligent Sla-gistics. You are now officially a very strange person.

JENNIFER MARCUS. Happy birthday Todd. I know I'm early … *(She reaches into her pocket, gives him a custom-made Rubik's cube.)*

TODD. Dude. It's a cube!

JENNIFER MARCUS. Shake it.

TODD. *(Shaking the cube.)* Whoa, it changes color! Where did you get this?

JENNIFER MARCUS. I built it.

TODD. Dude. How cool.

JENNIFER MARCUS. It works just like a regular one. Try it. *(He starts manipulating it.)*

TODD. But it keeps changing colors.

JENNIFER MARCUS. Yeah, it's like a Rubik's cube wrapped in a ripple of time. So now you have to match all the colors but you have to do it at like, a precise moment in time.

TODD. Dude, I couldn't even do the one that had stickers on it.

JENNIFER MARCUS. It's more instinctual. It uses another part of the brain to figure it out.

TODD. Whoa.

JENNIFER MARCUS. Don't think so much.

TODD. *(A la Yoda from* Star Wars.*)* Use the Force, Todd. Trust your feelings.

JENNIFER MARCUS. That's right.

TODD. Bitchin'. Thanks, Jen. *(Excitable underscoring back in.)*

JENNIFER MARCUS. *(To the audience.)* So it was all set up. I incorporated myself through the Calabasas Chamber of Commerce website, Colonel Hubbard sent me a contract at my new P.O. box. Todd delivered it to me, I sent it back and three days later I got my first package from Raytheon, a primitive gyroscope, some blueprints for the P-46 medium-range cruise missile and a complete systems schematic for the Margraff Communications Satellite orbiting high above the earth. It took me two whole days to redraw the guidance system and translate an extinct computer language into something reasonable, but I got it done. *(Lights up on Preston, looking at some blueprints.)*

PRESTON. Miss Marcus. I have to confess somethin'. They tell me we sending work to a bunch of Cali-fornians and I says to myself, o brother, Californians …

JENNIFER MARCUS. Is it okay? Do you guys like it?

PRESTON. See, I come from thinking says, California ain't gave us nothing worth a something exceptin' the avocado. And in Gray, Georgia, we ain't got the right kind of Mexicans to do anything about it, so we don't eat 'em …

JENNIFER MARCUS. The schematics, Preston. What about …

PRESTON. … So I have to confess. I was not a supporter, Miss Marcus. But we're a humble people.

JENNIFER MARCUS. Preston …

PRESTON. I'm a humble man, Miss Marcus.

JENNIFER MARCUS. I can see that.

PRESTON. I was wrong. I have wronged you.

JENNIFER MARCUS. So the work is good.

PRESTON. Itsa goddamn record for efficiency, I'll tell you that! I don't know what the hell it is, but that's not my job. Anyway the boys upstairs sure like it!

JENNIFER MARCUS. Awesome.

PRESTON. We'll be sending you all that stuff you requested. We got some friends at NASA been working on robots and stuff. You know that Neil Armstrong fella, done walked on the moon? *(Looks around, then:)* Android.

JENNIFER MARCUS. O-kay.

PRESTON. You didn't hear that from me. We also gonna send you more work, if that's okay. You're really making my job easier, Miss Marcus. I'm beginning to have … special feelings. *(Lights down on Preston.)*

JENNIFER MARCUS. *(She sprays the computer with disinfectant. To the audience.)* Ew. Okay, so that was … *mostly* going good. Of course, yeah, as you can see I was also doing a few other things. And really you have to blame it on my obsessive streak. What else would make a girl start hacking into a Department of Defense guidance satellite? I mean, really, it's not normal, but ya know, if it's there, right in front of you … I'm sending you a series of designs for a programmable mannequin with self-navigational abilities. *(We hear a "bling" noise from the computer. To the audience.)* Study the designs, bounty hunter. Look for weaknesses, not that you're going to find them. You're going to need to know what Jenny can do. It took some time in the beginning, but after the first breakthrough … *(Music out. Lights up on Dr. Yakunin in his office and Jennifer's bedroom. A frustrated Jennifer sits at her computer, lit by her computer screen. On her bed is a robotic arm with a line of cable connecting back to the computer. Jennifer keeps typing in things and looking back at the arm.)*

DR. YAKUNIN. You can't get anything but Thai food in this city! I go to one of them yesterday afternoon, waitress tells me, eat this. Okay I say. Eight hours later where am I? WHERE AM I? I'm on my bathroom floor, clutching my stomach …

JENNIFER MARCUS. Dr. Yakunin.

DR. YAKUNIN. … dry-heaving, shooting out of both ends!

JENNIFER MARCUS. Okay, that's gross.

DR. YAKUNIN. Yes, but you are not the one with forty-foot tape worm writhing around in your intestines, are you? *(She goes to the arm, makes some adjustments.)*

JENNIFER MARCUS. There's something wrong with my design, Dr. Yakunin.

DR. YAKUNIN. Nothing wrong with design. I have looked at it myself.

JENNIFER MARCUS. I've been at it for three days now, goddamnit, it doesn't move.

DR. YAKUNIN. Design is fine. You have to trust me! *(She types more into the computer.)*

JENNIFER MARCUS. I'm a loser. I'm a total idiot. Forget it.

DR. YAKUNIN. Smart girl, no give up. This is horseshit!

JENNIFER MARCUS. I'm no good at it anymore.

DR. YAKUNIN. Cheap bullshit. Victim shit. You need to stop whining like a little Roschenmeyer and focus!

JENNIFER MARCUS. It's been three days.

DR. YAKUNIN. Oh yes, of course, three days. It takes me fifteen years, FIFTEEN YEARS of writing theory, everyone laughing at me. *(She talks directly into her computer camera.)*

JENNIFER MARCUS. Your theories were genius.

DR. YAKUNIN. But dead as ass meat until you come along and prove them. I walk around entire convention center, stupid idiot science fair, kids with idiot volcano and tulip displays. But what is this girl, sitting piggy-nosed against a glass enclosure? What's she looking at so seriously? Two simple machines. One built, one in pieces.

JENNIFER MARCUS. Yeah, well, this is not a simple machine. *(She goes back to the arm, makes another adjustment, then back to the computer.)*

DR. YAKUNIN. Whole world at time, says, robots cannot think. Cannot learn. You? You leave dismantled parts scattered all over box. Robot wander around for hours, what is this? What is this gear? What is this wheel? *(She has her head in her hands, total frustration.)* We all gather around. We watch robot thinking. We watch it assemble, BUILD goddamnit, another robot right in front of us! You set off revolution in robotics. *(She hits one last button on the computer without looking up. Trembling, anticipatory underscoring begins to fade in.)* Everyone says it is fluke, teenage girl proves cognitive artificial intelligence. *(Suddenly the arm reaches up. Then does numbers, one, two, three, four, five.)* No way, cannot happen. Yet secretly, they all take up where you leave off. Design is fine. Turn around, Jennifer. *(Jennifer looks back.)*

41

JENNIFER MARCUS. Oh boy! *(She types something in. The arm acts like it's shaking hands.)* Yes!

DR. YAKUNIN. Try looping the two sequences together. *(She types something else in, the arm does numbers, one, two, three, four, five, then shakes hands.)* Mr. Spock. *(She types something in, then the arm does a Vulcan hello.)* The Roschenmeyer. *(She types something in, the arm extends its middle finger.)* Fuck you too, Mr. Arm! Congratulations, Jennifer! I think we have progress! *(Lights down on Dr. Yakunin. The music swells. Jennifer walks over to the hand, giggling. She nervously touches it. It flinches. She gives it a high-five, it gives her one back but does not let go, feeling all the contours of her hand.)*

JENNIFER MARCUS. *(Shouting.)* OH, BABY!

ADELE HARTWICK. *(Offstage.)* Jennifer! We are trying to get some sleep.

JENNIFER MARCUS. *(Trying not to laugh.)* Sorry, Mom. *(Jennifer walks toward the audience. Leaving the arm in the background, music fades back to underscoring. To the audience.)* Okay, so I'm fucking cool. And I'm having like a great time. And really, it couldn't have gone better. *(Todd enters with a box. Then exits. To the audience.)* Todd would deliver new parts almost every other day, I would give him the stuff for Raytheon … *(Cardboard boxes, a crate, blueprints, etc., begin to appear throughout Jennifer's room. The robotic arm rises from the bed, exposing the actor playing the robot. She sits at the end of the bed, the cable still attached to the computer. To the audience.)* … and trying my best to avoid my parents, and thank God for their own private little worlds, ya know, I spent most of my time building the robot, piece by piece. But, of course, I forgot to take out the garbage and ya know, she got word from her job about another acquisition and well … *(Adele enters dragging a garbage can outside the house.)*

ADELE HARTWICK. So from now on you are living by a new constitution. As long as you live rent-free in this house, these are the rules and there's no discussion. GOT IT?!

JENNIFER MARCUS. GOT IT!

MR. MARCUS. *(Offstage.)* Is the screaming over with for the night? *(Adele exits. Jennifer types something on her computer. The robot's head snaps to attention, talking very fast.)*

THE ROBOT. Hello. My name is Jenni-fer Marcus. I am twentee-too years old. I live in Calaba-sas, California. My parents are Marsh-all Marcus and A-dele Har-twick. My favorite color is zuma blue.

JENNIFER MARCUS. No, it's not. *(She types into her computer. The robot's head tilts back and then snaps forward.)*

THE ROBOT. I live in Calaba-sas, California. My parents are Marsh-all Marcus and A-dele Har-twick. My favorite co-lor is sunset red. It makes me happy. And one day I hope to paint my house that co-lor.

ADELE HARTWICK. *(Offstage.)* So that means she's going to get a job. And that means you are going to arrive at that job, ON TIME, Jennifer.

JENNIFER MARCUS. I am Jennifer Marcus.

THE ROBOT. I am Jen-ni-fer Mar-cus.

ADELE HARTWICK. *(Offstage.)* Because the time of living off of your parents is over.

JENNIFER MARCUS. I am twenty-two years old.

THE ROBOT. I am twenty-two years old.

ADELE HARTWICK. *(Offstage.)* Maybe you could answer me. Maybe you could pretend like you were listening to me.

JENNIFER MARCUS. *(Fiercely.)* I hear you.

THE ROBOT. *(Doubly fiercely.)* I hear you.

ADELE HARTWICK. *(Offstage.)* I don't think I like that tone of voice. Maybe you could try that again?

JENNIFER MARCUS. Dear Mother Hartwick. I not only hear you I wholeheartedly agree with you. It's time I got a job, it's time I made something of myself.

ADELE HARTWICK. *(Offstage.)* If you're trying to piss me off, Jennifer, you're failing.

THE ROBOT. Mother Hart-wickee. I not only hear you … *(Jennifer types into the computer. The robot's body and voice both sag down.)* I hole-heart-ily aggggreeeee wwwiiittttthhhh yooooouuuu …

JENNIFER MARCUS. What the hell do you want me to say? I'll get a goddamn job.

ADELE HARTWICK. *(Offstage.)* You're gonna go out this week and find a job?

JENNIFER MARCUS. I will find a job.

ADELE HARTWICK. *(Offstage.)* This week? *(Jennifer types on the computer. The robot snaps her head and body back into full attention.)*

JENNIFER MARCUS. I am Jennifer.

THE ROBOT. I am Jenni-fer.

ADELE HARTWICK. *(Offstage, loud.)* I am waiting, Jennifer.

JENNIFER MARCUS. I am Jennifer Marcus.

THE ROBOT. *(Finally echoing.)* I am Jennifer Marcus.

ADELE HARTWICK. *(Offstage.)* JENNIFER!

MR. MARCUS. *(Offstage.)* Jennifer, answer your …

JENNIFER MARCUS. THIS WEEK. YES!

THE ROBOT. THIS WEEK. YES!

ADELE HARTWICK. *(Offstage.)* And if that's not the case young lady, you are going to hate your life. So help me God, Jennifer, you are going to hate it. *(We hear the sound of a door slamming. Jennifer types into the computer.)*

THE ROBOT. I am Jennifer Marcus. I am twenty-two years old. *(Jennifer types something into the computer.)*

JENNIFER MARCUS. I am Jenniff …

THE ROBOT. I am Jenniff. *(Jennifer hits a button on her computer. The robot freezes. Jennifer looks back at her door, then turns back to the robot. A moment.)*

JENNIFER MARCUS. I am Jenny.

THE ROBOT. I am Jenny.

JENNIFER MARCUS. I am Jenny Chow.

THE ROBOT. I am Jenny Chow.

JENNIFER MARCUS. I was born in a mud hut in China.

THE ROBOT. I was born in a mud hut in China.

JENNIFER MARCUS. And my mother loved me so much she gave me away.

THE ROBOT. And my mother loved me so much she gave me away. *(Jennifer types into her computer. The robot's head falls down, the body freezes. Jennifer types furiously into her computer. After a moment, she stops typing, looks to the robot, then touches one button on the computer. The robot sits up. Its voice is now wonderfully human-sounding.)*

JENNY CHOW. *(Formerly known as The Robot.)* My name is Jenny Chow. I am twenty-two years old. I was born in a mud hut in China and my mother loved me so much she gave me away. *(The same trembling, anticipatory music fades up. The robot looks at the cable in her arm. She rips it out and then rises to her feet! She is standing!)* I live in Calabasas, California but this is not my home. I have one friend named Todd and he is very nice. I am Jenny Chow and I am very beautiful and I want to see the world. *(She turns to face Jennifer, extends her arm.)* It is very nice to meet you. *(Jenny chow smiles. Blackout.)*

End of Act One

ACT TWO

We hear the music from the end of Act One, only an amped-up, rocked-out version of it. The music abruptly cuts out on the first sight of Jennifer Marcus standing next to a fully dressed Jenny Chow, clothed directly from Jennifer's personal closet.

JENNIFER MARCUS. *(To the audience.)* Yeah, it was getting pretty cool. And Dr. Yakunin's theory on instinctual programming was so right. And like, almost, ya know, immediately, Jenny was taking on her own personality. Actually, she was turning out to be a lot like me, curious, excitable, poor sportsmanship, but whatever, who cares, the big thing was when I wasn't looking, she was beginning to make her own decisions. With guidance, she was becoming beautiful. I sketched a design for a more streamlined rapid response delivery system for the P-46 and Preston was beside himself. He sent me the rest of Jenny's body and some virtual reality gloves, feet, and goggles. Simultaneously, I was also hard at work on the propulsion and navigational device, modeled after the good ol' P-46. It was still a bitch keeping it under the radar at the house, but really, you wouldn't believe it, the acquisition fell through and Mom was trying to be cool for once, I mean really trying. *(Quietly, we hear a bubble gum pop classic like "Saturday Night" by the Bay City Rollers.* * *To the audience.)* Her and my dad were even going out on dates. The house was starting to breathe again and I, yeah, in those few moments when I got some sleep, I was dreaming of reunion in China. *(The song volume rises, flooding the theater with good feelings as we watch Jenny Chow evolve. We see Jennifer Marcus, wearing her virtual gloves and feet moving her hands back and forth over her knees, first like a game of pattycake, then like the Charleston. Jenny Chow mimics her actions. Blackout/light change.*

Lights up. Todd skateboards onstage with a pizza box. He flips open the box and on the inside it reads May twenty-sixth. Blackout/light change.

* See Special Note on Songs and Recordings on copyright page.

Lights up. Jennifer Marcus hands Jenny Chow books to speed-read through. The first book is Anne of Green Gables, *then* Das Kapital, *then* Kama Sutra. *Jenny Chow really likes* Kama Sutra. *Blackout/light change.*

Lights up on Todd holding a pizza box. He looks over to Adele, also onstage, talking on her cell phone. Mr. Marcus comes up from behind her wearing a chef's hat, an apron and carrying an egg scrambler. He silently mimics Adele talking on the phone [blah, blah, blah]. She tries to brush him away and he gooses her with the scrambler. She hangs up her phone and he backs off, whipping off his apron, using it as a matador's cape. Adele pretends to be a bull, takes her fingers and makes two little horns on the top of her head, then makes one of her feet out to be a hoof, kicking up dirt. She charges after Mr. Marcus, who turns in mock fright and heads for the bedroom for a little afternoon ah yeah. Todd opens up his pizza box to reveal the date June fourth. Blackout/light change.

Lights up. Jennifer Marcus and Jenny Chow playing a game of checkers. Jennifer Marcus jumps all of Jenny Chow's pieces. Jennifer celebrates and Jenny Chow chokes her with one hand. Jennifer drags herself over to the computer, hits one button and Jenny Chow releases her. Jennifer shakes her head then goes back to typing. Blackout/light change.

Lights up on Todd holding a pizza box. We see Dr. Yakunin reading a "Jenny Project" report on the toilet. He reaches for some toilet paper, but this is New Haven, so there is none. He rips out one page from the report, shaking his head ... Todd opens up the pizza box as soon as he can, revealing the date, June twelfth. Blackout/light change.

Lights up. We see Jennifer Marcus with her virtual reality gloves on again. Jenny Chow is holding Jennifer's old mascot pom-poms. They both do an elaborate choreographed cheer and then Jennifer falls back on her bed, forgetting to take off her gloves and feet. Jenny Chow falls out the window, disappearing. Jennifer's head looks up from the bed, out the window. After a second we see Jenny Chow's head, then upper torso hovering in the window. As the music fades, we hear the sound of a muffled rocket engine. To the audience.) And so, uh-huh, I totally forgot to take off my gloves and feet and she fell right out the window. But, of course, isn't that how we got penicillin? And really, what was totally amazing about my fuck-up was Jenny's reaction. Here was Dr. Yakunin's revised automata hierarchy proved. At the top of the pyramid is self-preservation. *(Lights fade on the window and Jenny. To the audience.)* Facing destruction, Jenny chose to use her untested, very experimental propulsion mechanism to save herself. We were way ahead of the curve. And we were, like, ready for the last big test. June nineteenth, a trial run. *(Lights up on Todd in his car wearing a head-set cell phone. Jennifer talks from her bedroom computer. She is setting up a mini-control center. Jenny Chow is sitting in the back seat staring at Todd. Todd looks at her in rearview mirror, a little paranoid.)*

TODD. Jennifer? Hel-lo, Jennifer?

JENNIFER MARCUS. Todd?

TODD. Jennifer. Yeah, I'm here.

JENNIFER MARCUS. Gimme a second, Todd.

TODD. Okay, man. But, like, your robot is beginning to freak me out a bit.

JENNIFER MARCUS. Call her Jenny.

TODD. Fine, so she's like staring at me like I have a stash on me or something and I don't. And …

JENNIFER MARCUS. And what, Todd?

TODD. Well, actually I do have a stash and I might have smoked some of it before I came by your house and my usual source was out, so I got some of the gnarly neighborhood weed at Leo's and its doing some fairly bogus things with my head. *(Jennifer puts on her wired-up gloves. Jenny Chow responds by lunging her hands forward. Todd jumps up in his seat.)* Ah shit! She just fucking moved on me!

JENNIFER MARCUS. Take it easy.

TODD. She's totally out of control!

JENNIFER MARCUS. I'm putting on my gloves, Todd.

TODD. This is no good. No way! No good can come from this. *(Jennifer starts wiggling her fingers. Jenny Chow mimics.)*

JENNIFER MARCUS. Relax.

TODD. Ah, come on! She's wiggling her fingers now. Can she *not* do that?

JENNIFER MARCUS. Todd, she's doing what I'm doing.

TODD. Cyborgs are bad news. They're always supposed to be our friends and then they fucking turn on you.

JENNIFER MARCUS. Let me get my goggles on.

TODD. C3PO. That's the only cool one. *(Jennifer puts her goggles on.)* I'm gonna fucking kill Leo.

JENNIFER MARCUS. Turn around, I want to see you. How much pot did you smoke? *(Todd turns back to his seat.)*

TODD. Alright, I don't think I'm ready for a just-say-no right now, okay? I've hardly seen you in over a month, you don't return my calls and suddenly it's like, hey Todd, could you come over and drive my ROBOT around? I mean, C'MON, MAN!

JENNIFER MARCUS. Where are you?

TODD. *(Trying to calm down.)* Whatever, I'm at the top of Valley Circle.

JENNIFER MARCUS. Good. Alright, cool. Cool, alright, gimme a second, I got to wait for the satellite to kick in. *(Jennifer is stretching. Jenny Chow is doing the same thing in the backseat.)*

TODD. I can't believe you have a satellite and you're giving me shit about smoking pot. *(To Jenny, meekly.)* Could you please be more like a human girl?

JENNIFER MARCUS. She's not programmed to listen to you, Todd.

TODD. What are we even doing here? I gotta be back at Amechi's in an hour.

JENNIFER MARCUS. Just wait. Jenny, I want you to thank Todd for driving you and then we're going to get out of the car.

JENNY CHOW. Todd you are very nice for the drive. You are cool of many ways.

TODD. *(Shaking his head.)* Okay, thanks.

JENNIFER MARCUS. We're still working on grammar. *(Jennifer mimes opening the car door and Jenny Chow actually does it. We hear the quiet beginnings of some excitable music.)*

TODD. She can't talk good, she can't hear me but she can open a car door.

JENNIFER MARCUS. Jenny, walk a safe distance from the car and stop. *(Jenny Chow follows the directions.)*

TODD. I think I have to question your priorities here.

JENNIFER MARCUS. We've been busy working on other things. Isn't that right, Jenny?

JENNY CHOW. We've been working on other things.

JENNIFER MARCUS. Are you ready, Todd?

TODD. Ready for what?

JENNIFER MARCUS. Turn on your car.

TODD. What?

JENNIFER MARCUS. Put your totally souped-up Dodge Dart Swinger into gear and step on the accelerator.

TODD. You just want me to leave her here?

JENNIFER MARCUS. Yes.

TODD. Whatever. *(Todd turns on the ignition.)* This is *so* not the Friday night I wanted.

JENNIFER MARCUS. You still say you're the best driver in San Fernando Valley, Todd? *(Jennifer squats then raises her head, Jenny*

Chow mimics.)
TODD. Yeah.
JENNIFER MARCUS. Prove it. Jenny. Go. *(Jennifer Marcus raises up, quickly throwing her hands straight up in the air. We hear a big swoosh sound. Jenny Chow takes off. Shouting!)* Whhhhheeeeee-eeeeewwwwwwwwwwwwwwwwwwwwwwwhhhhhhhhoooooooooo! Haaaaaaaaaaaaaaaaaa!
TODD. *(Wowed.)* Dude. *(Jennifer Marcus throws her arms out to the side. Jenny zooms offstage. Totally wowed.)* Dude!
JENNIFER MARCUS. Can you see her?
TODD. Whoa!
JENNIFER MARCUS. Todd! *(A half-size Jenny Chow rockets across the stage!)*
TODD. Fucking A!
JENNIFER MARCUS. TODD!
TODD. What?!
JENNIFER MARCUS. You okay?
TODD. Dude.
JENNIFER MARCUS. Todd?
TODD. I *should not* have done all that weed. *(Jennifer Marcus begins turning in a circle. A quarter-size Jenny Chow miniature outside Jennifer's window!)*
JENNIFER MARCUS. You've got to follow her.
TODD. *(Repeating her.)* I've got to follow her.
JENNIFER MARCUS. Now!
TODD. Huh? Oh, right. Okay! *(He totally steps on the accelerator, flooring it! Jennifer stops turning, quarter-size Jenny Chow flies past window again!)*
JENNIFER MARCUS. I don't know how long I can keep her up in the air! This might not last long!
TODD. What do you mean?!
JENNIFER MARCUS. I mean I don't know how long our energy source goes for! Do you see her? *(Half-size Jenny Chow flies across stage!)*
TODD. Yeah, I can see her!
JENNIFER MARCUS. Good! Good! I'm flying over Woodlake Avenue.
TODD. Okay, cool! This is cool! *(He turns the wheel sharply.)*
JENNIFER MARCUS. Just take Valley Circle ... *(A stop sign flies by.)*
TODD. Okay, shit! That was a stop sign.

JENNIFER MARCUS. Make a right at Burbank! *(A mailbox tumbles by.)*

TODD. Okay, that was a mailbox!

JENNIFER MARCUS. Then a left at Mariano …

TODD. Dude. Bobcats! *(A pack of bobcats runs past the car, the last one hits the car and goes airborne.)* Sorry, man. *(He makes another sharp right-hand turn.)*

JENNIFER MARCUS. C'mon, Todd, Jenny is getting bored! Isn't that right, Jenny?! *(Jenny Chow [the actor] shoots across stage!)*

JENNY CHOW. Jennyyyyy boredddddd.

TODD. Oh, is that right?! Well, I'm coming right under her.

JENNIFER MARCUS. I see you. Can you see us now? *(Jennifer Marcus lunges forward with her hands. Half-size Jenny Chow swoops across stage!)*

JENNIFER MARCUS and JENNY CHOW. Whhhheeeeeeee-eeeewwwwwwwww!

TODD. Whhhhooooooaaaaa! *(Todd looks ahead.)*

JENNIFER MARCUS. The greatest driver in the west Valley?!

TODD. Where the fuck are you?

JENNIFER MARCUS. Towards Ventura. We'll wait for you. *(Jennifer circles again. Quarter-size Jenny Chow whooshes past Jennifer's window.)*

TODD. How the fuck did you do this?

JENNIFER MARCUS. It's what I've been doing for the last month.

TODD. For the month?! Jenny, man, that is a *flying girl.* It took you a month to make a flying girl?!

JENNIFER MARCUS. You should apply yourself sometime.

TODD. Dude, one time it took me a month to make *a bong.* It wasn't even functional, man.

JENNIFER MARCUS. I have a friend at the Department of Defense, another friend at Raytheon.

TODD. They built it for you? How did you pay for it?

JENNIFER MARCUS. I suck their dicks. I make sucky-fucky with them.

TODD. Ya know … *(Jenny Chow [the actor] sweeps across stage, hovers there.)*

JENNY CHOW. I make sucky-fuckyyyyyyyyyyy.

JENNIFER MARCUS. Jenny, no. Delete that! I made her, Todd. I made her myself. I fix stuff for people, they pay me back with old parts. I'm really good at it.

TODD. We'll see about that. Race you to Serrania Park.

JENNIFER MARCUS. Where's Serrania Park?!

TODD. Ask your satellite! *(He floors it. His car moves forward. She takes off one of her gloves. One of Jenny's arms fall. She begins to spin out of control while Jennifer types into the computer.)*

JENNIFER MARCUS. *(Typing it in.)* Serrania Park.

TODD. Ya know, Jenny, you've got to get out more.

JENNIFER MARCUS. C'mon. *(She puts back on her gloves. Jenny straightens out.)*

TODD. *(Getting smug.)* Too much time with technology, not enough time with the people.

JENNIFER MARCUS. Got it. I got it! You're gone! *(Jennifer squats down and then thrusts up and forward! Jenny Chow rockets ahead! Todd turns his wheel!)*

JENNY CHOW. Oh no.

JENNIFER MARCUS. Oh shit. *(Jennifer begins looking at her glove, then her computer. Jenny begins to rattle, shake, then shoots offstage!)*

TODD. What? What's going on?

JENNIFER MARCUS. I'm losing her, Todd.

TODD. Oh shit! Okay.

JENNIFER MARCUS. I got to land her.

TODD. There's a pool at the park. Aim for the pool.

JENNIFER MARCUS. Okay, okay.

TODD. Okay, I see you. *(He slams on the brakes. Half-size Jenny Chow flies past Todd.)* Dude, just went over me.

JENNIFER MARCUS. Oh, God. I'm coming down!

TODD. Whoaaaaaaaaaaaaaaaaaaaaaaa!

JENNY CHOW. Whoooooooaaaaaaaaaaaaaaaaaaaaaaaaa!

JENNIFER, JENNY and TODD. Aaaaaaaaaaaaooooooooooo-oooooooooooooooooooooooooooooooooooooo! *(We hear the sound of trees splintering, then a muffled crash, some water.)*

TODD. Dude! *(Some water is splashed on Todd.)*

JENNIFER MARCUS. Did we get water? Todd, did we hit water?

TODD. Dude.

JENNIFER MARCUS. Todd?

TODD. Now that's a fucking cannonball!

JENNIFER MARCUS. *(Pause, a big sigh of relief.)* Todd?

TODD. Here.

JENNIFER MARCUS. Can you swim?

TODD. I'm on it. *(Lights fade as Todd walks after Jenny. Lights up on Jennifer back at her computer. She is simultaneously typing and working on a small wristwatch.)*

JENNIFER MARCUS. *(To the audience.)* So I got Preston to send me some waterproof plastique moldings used for amputee appendages ... *(We hear a "blip" noise from the computer. To the audience.)* What? No, I don't know how you're supposed to track down a flying robot. That's not my job. You're the bounty hunter. She flies — Deal with it. *(We hear a "blip" noise from the computer. To the audience.)* Right, so look, I was wild busy making my virtual reality controls obsolete. I did diagnostic work for a "weather satellite" and got back an experimental microprocessor. And almost to the hour that I had Jenny talking with my wristwatch ... *(Jennifer talks into her watch.)* Jenny begin yoga stretches ... *(Jenny Chow enters and begins to do yoga poses behind Jennifer.)* I got an instant message from Shanghai. *(Lights up on Terrence.)*

TERRENCE. I found her, Jennifer. I found Chow Su Yang.

JENNIFER MARCUS. Terrence, you're the best.

TERRENCE. Actually, her name is Zhang Su Yang, now. She got married eighteen years ago. She's living in Dongtai, a few hours north of Shanghai. Here's her address. *(We hear a "boink" noise from the computer.)*

JENNIFER MARCUS. Got it. Alright, for this you get the tits. A nice set ... *(Jennifer begins to take off her shirt.)*

TERRENCE. Don't. Listen. They're sending me back home, Jennifer. I asked them to.

JENNIFER MARCUS. Oh, but that's great. You can come visit me.

TERRENCE. No. Um, no. I need to reestablish my relationship with God. You see, I can't talk to you anymore. I mean, don't get me wrong. I loved doing this for you. I did.

JENNIFER MARCUS. *(Very sincere.)* You'll never know, ya know, how grateful I am.

TERRENCE. You changed my life forever and I don't know if that's a good thing. I've got to go. Good luck, Jennifer. *(Lights down on Terrence. Jennifer sits back for a second, then begins to type.)*

JENNIFER MARCUS. Dear Terrence, I'm glad to hear about your decision. I think it's the right one, okay. I don't believe in your god, you know that. But I think if He did exist, He'd be really pleased with you. Thank you so much Terrence, and in case you're really serious about never talking to me again, I just wanted to say, you're like, the sexiest Mormon I've ever known. Smiley face. *(She smiles.)* Your sister in the celestial kingdom, Jennifer. *(She presses a key on the computer and we hear a "bling" noise. To the audience.)* We were really ready to go on July fourteenth but there had been some bad weather up around the Aleutian Islands. Luckily, there had been an arsonist lighting up enough Molotovs to keep my father busy on the balcony but my mother was coming home from another road trip on the seventeenth. And, you know, I had this sense, I don't know, that I was only going to get away with this for so much longer. So, July sixteenth. Three days ago. *(Jenny Chow rises up from her Dog Rising to Sun or Cow Giving Birth to Chicken whatever yoga pose. Jennifer Marcus is holding the silk scarf.)* Do you know what this is?

JENNY CHOW. It is red and black and yellow and …

JENNIFER MARCUS. It's a scarf.

JENNY CHOW. It is a scarf. I like scarf.

JENNIFER MARCUS. Here. *(Jenny Chow holds it out in front of her.)* You wear it around your neck. Look. *(She ties it around Jenny Chow's neck.)* The last time you saw your mother, she left this with you. It's very special to her. She asked for it back. That's why I built … That's why you're going tonight. To give Su Yang something she lost a long time age.

JENNY CHOW. Oh. Very special. Okay. It feels nice on my fingers.

JENNIFER MARCUS. Yeah. It does. *(We hear excitable underscoring.)* Are you ready? Are you excited?

JENNY CHOW. I am Jenny Chow. I am very excited.

JENNIFER MARCUS. In Mandarin?

JENNY CHOW. *(In Mandarin.)* Wo shi Chow Jenny. Wo fei chang xing fen.

JENNIFER MARCUS. I hope that's right. Alright. Be good. *(She walks Jenny over to the window. Into her watch.)* Dongtai, China. Go. *(Jenny Chow climbs out the window and disappears. We hear a "swooooosssh" sound. To the audience.)* In order to save time and fuel, I configured the Margraff Satellite to guide Jenny up the coast of California and then up through the stratosphere, reentering above North Korea. She would follow a slipstream over the Yangtze River and touch down in Dongtai. We would be out of contact for six hours and the waiting, ya know, it like started me thinking. Was I forgetting anything? I had a powerful microphone rigged to Jenny's head. I had a Chinese to English voice translator ready to go on the computer. I *had* thought of everything. But in those six hours, I thought of some things I had forgotten. Like what was I going to say? What did I want to hear? *(We hear a phone ring, music fades. Lights up on Adele with her laptop on a tray in front of her. The laptop is closed. She is holding an air-*

phone. To the audience.) I mean, I had been so caught up in doing it, I hadn't like even asked, why? *(Jennifer picks up her phone.)* Hello?

ADELE HARTWICK. Hi. It's me.

JENNIFER MARCUS. Hi. Where are you?

ADELE HARTWICK. In a plane.

JENNIFER MARCUS. Oh.

ADELE HARTWICK. Isn't it incredible they can make a phone that works from the plane?

JENNIFER MARCUS. *(Pause.)* Yeah. *(Pause.)* I'll get Dad.

ADELE HARTWICK. No, don't. Wait.

JENNIFER MARCUS. What?

ADELE HARTWICK. What are you up to?

JENNIFER MARCUS. Oh, nothing.

ADELE HARTWICK. Nothing?

JENNIFER MARCUS. Just working on the computer. *(Adele hesitates, sees her closed laptop. Gets an idea.)*

ADELE HARTWICK. I'm having trouble with my laptop.

JENNIFER MARCUS. What's the matter with it?

ADELE HARTWICK. It uh … froze, up on me. The idiots in IT keep telling me it's my fault.

JENNIFER MARCUS. Just hit control/alt/delete and if that doesn't work there's a tiny button in the back, you can tap it with a pen and that'll reset it.

ADELE HARTWICK. Oh. *(Adele waits, pretends she is rebooting.)* Thanks. You were right.

JENNIFER MARCUS. You don't have to thank me.

ADELE HARTWICK. I mean about her. I mean I don't know if you're right but you could be. That could be her real name. If they didn't write in the father's name, why would they write in the mom's name? It doesn't make sense, does it? I think it's something they told us to tell you if you ever asked. I guess they don't want thousands of girls bombarding the countryside looking for their moms. No wait. That's not true either.

JENNIFER MARCUS. Mom?

ADELE HARTWICK. We didn't know what to say when you were young so … you just make something up. They don't tell you anything. They just hand you a baby and that's it. I didn't even remember I was lying. I have no idea what she did. How could I? *(Pause.)* I just wanted you to know that.

JENNIFER MARCUS. Oh.

ADELE HARTWICK. I got you something. There's a mall by the

54

hotel and …

JENNY CHOW. Jennifer Marcus. *(Lights up on Jenny Chow. Her shoulder looks like its been struck by lightning.)*

JENNIFER MARCUS. *(Into her watch.)* Hold on.

JENNY CHOW. Jennifer Marcus.

ADELE HARTWICK. Online?

JENNIFER MARCUS. No. I was …

ADELE HARTWICK. Thanks for the computer help.

JENNIFER MARCUS. *(Pause.)* Sure.

ADELE HARTWICK. I'll see you later tonight. *(Adele hangs up the phone. Lights out on Adele.)*

JENNIFER MARCUS. Mom? *(Jennifer hangs up her phone.)*

JENNY CHOW. Jennifer Marcus.

JENNIFER MARCUS. *(Into her watch.)* Jenny?

JENNY CHOW. I feel dirt. I am Jenny!

JENNIFER MARCUS. You're okay?

JENNY CHOW. There was fire in the clouds. Some of it got on my clothes.

JENNIFER MARCUS. Must have been that electrical storm. Sorry.

JENNY CHOW. It was very beautiful.

JENNIFER MARCUS. Where are you, Jenny?

JENNY CHOW. Jenny is in Dongtai. Walking to my mother's house. *(Music fades in. Lights up on Su Yang, Mr. Zhang, and a boy, sitting at a table. [The actors playing Adele, Mr. Marcus, and Todd will play these parts.] They are eating dinner. Mr. Zhang is reading a newspaper.)*

JENNIFER MARCUS. *(Into her watch.)* Oh wow.

JENNY CHOW. I can see it now. It is not a mud hut. But it is not like Ca-la-basas. It is … shorter.

JENNIFER MARCUS. *(Into her watch.)* What do you see?

JENNY CHOW. I see family sitting around a table. There is a man, a boy, a beautiful lady. They are eating dinner. *(Jennifer puts on her wired-up goggles.)*

JENNIFER MARCUS. *(Into her watch.)* There's a boy?

JENNY CHOW. Yes, a boy. There is a man, a boy, a beautiful lady.

JENNIFER MARCUS. *(Into her watch.)* Are you okay? *(Jenny Chow circles around the family, as if she is walking around the house.)*

JENNY CHOW. I am fine. The house is wrapped in wood, and concrete. I am looking through windows. *(Su Yang looks up from the table. Did she hear something?)* I see a man, a boy, a beautiful lady.

JENNIFER MARCUS. *(Into the watch.)* I see them too. Jenny, go to the front door. *(Jenny Chow walks to the front door.)*

JENNY CHOW. I am at front door.

JENNIFER MARCUS. *(Into her watch.)* I know.

JENNY CHOW. The door is wrapped in wood.

JENNIFER MARCUS. *(Into her watch.)* I see that.

JENNY CHOW. Jennifer?

JENNIFER MARCUS. *(Into her watch.)* Gimme a second.

JENNY CHOW. *(Beat.)* That was a second.

JENNIFER MARCUS. *(Into her watch.)* Hold on. *(Jennifer Marcus takes a deep breath. Readies herself, then ... Into her watch.)* Okay, Jenny. I want you to knock on the door, then take a few steps back out of the light, okay?

JENNY CHOW. O-kay. *(Jenny Chow knocks on the door, then moves back. The heads of the family turn to the door. Music fades out.)*

MR. ZHANG. *(In Mandarin.)* Ni qu kai men. [You go open door.] *(Mr. Zhang returns to his newspaper. Su Yang dabs her face with a cloth, then gets up and goes to the door. She straightens out her clothes and opens the door.)*

SU YANG. *(In Mandarin.)* Ni hao? [Hello?]

JENNIFER MARCUS. *(Into her watch.)* Turn on your translator, Jenny. *(Jenny Chow moves her head to her shoulder, then looks back at Su Yang. [Note: The Voice Translator should sound calming, gentle, and it should overlap near the end of Su Yang's lines.])*

SU YANG. *(In Mandarin.)* Ni hao?

VOICE TRANSLATOR FROM COMPUTER. Hello.

JENNY CHOW. I am to find Zhang Su Yang.

SU YANG. *(In Mandarin.)* Wo shi zhang tai tai, ni shi shui?

VOICE TRANSLATOR FROM COMPUTER. I am Mrs. Zhang. Who are you?

JENNY CHOW. Zhang Su Yang. Who was once, Chow — Su — Yang? *(Su Yang steps out to get a better look at Jenny.)*

SU YANG. *(In Mandarin.)* You xum mo shi?

VOICE TRANSLATOR FROM COMPUTER. What do you want?

JENNIFER MARCUS. *(Into her watch.)* Give her the scarf, Jenny. *(Jenny Chow walks to Su Yang, hands her the beautiful silk scarf, then backs away. Jennifer Marcus sits up in her chair, waiting. Su Yang looks at the scarf for a while, then something happens. Her eyes grow wide and she suddenly looks up at Jenny Chow. She stares at Jenny in disbelief, then covers her mouth with one hand. Su Yang starts crying.)*

Into her watch.) Talk to her, Jenny.

JENNY CHOW. O-kay. I am Jenny. I came from America. There was fire in the clouds … *(Su Yang slowly starts to walk toward Jenny.)*

JENNIFER MARCUS. *(Into her watch.)* C'mon Jenny … I am twenty-two years old.

JENNY CHOW. I am twenty-two years old. I live over the ocean and I was a good student. Many people think I am smart. *(Su Yang starts touching Jenny Chow everywhere. She is weeping uncontrollably.)*

JENNIFER MARCUS. *(Into her watch.)* I have been thinking about you for a long time.

JENNY CHOW. I have been thinking about you for a long time.

JENNIFER MARCUS. *(Into her watch.)* I have always wondered who you were. What you were like.

JENNY CHOW. I have wondered who you were. Always what you were like.

JENNIFER MARCUS. *(Into her watch.)* You gave me to a very nice family.

JENNY CHOW. You gave me to a very nice family.

JENNIFER MARCUS. *(Into her watch.)* I have had a very happy life so far.

JENNY CHOW. I have had a very happy life. So far. *(Su Yang backs away, trying to get ahold of herself.)*

MR. ZHANG. *(In Mandarin.)* Su Yang!

SU YANG. *(In Mandarin.)* Oh bu.

VOICE TRANSLATOR FROM COMPUTER. Oh no. *(Mr. Zhang puts down his newspaper, walks to the door.)*

MR. ZHANG. *(In Mandarin.)* Ni zhai zhe li gan ma?

VOICE TRANSLATOR FROM COMPUTER. What are you doing out here?

SU YANG. *(In Mandarin.)* Mei shi.

VOICE TRANSLATOR FROM COMPUTER. It is okay.

MR. ZHANG. *(In Mandarin.)* Zhe nu hai shi shai?

VOICE TRANSLATOR FROM COMPUTER. Who is this girl?

SU YANG. *(In Mandarin.)* Mei shi. Wo ma shang jing lai.

VOICE TRANSLATOR FROM COMPUTER. It is okay. I will be in soon. *(Mr. Zhang looks at Jenny Chow, then goes back inside his house, closing the door behind him.)*

SU YANG. *(In Mandarin.)* Ni shi zhum me lai de?

VOICE TRANSLATOR FROM COMPUTER. How did you get here?

JENNY CHOW. *(Pause.)* I flew.

SU YANG. *(In Mandarin.) Chuo fei ji?*

VOICE TRANSLATOR FROM COMPUTER. On airplane?

JENNY CHOW. I am a bird. I am Jenny Chow.

SU YANG. *(In Mandarin.) Ni zhum me zhao dao wo de?*

VOICE TRANSLATOR FROM COMPUTER. How did you find me?

JENNIFER MARCUS. *(Into her watch.)* I looked very hard. For a long time.

JENNY CHOW. For longest time, I look for you.

SU YANG. *(In Mandarin.) Ni de lian zhang ying le?*

VOICE TRANSLATOR FROM COMPUTER. Your face has grown hard.

JENNY CHOW. *(Pause.)* It is the wind. *(Pause.)* The wind chips away at me.

SU YANG. *(In Mandarin.) Ni xian zhai zhu na li?*

VOICE TRANSLATOR FROM COMPUTER. Where are you now?

JENNY CHOW. I live over the ocean. I live in America.

SU YANG. *(In Mandarin.) Ni zhuo xum me de?*

VOICE TRANSLATOR FROM COMPUTER. What do you do?

JENNIFER MARCUS. *(Into her watch.)* I like computers.

JENNY CHOW. I like computers. I like to play games. I like to dance with pom-poms.

SU YANG. *(In Mandarin.) Ni you ma ma?*

VOICE TRANSLATOR FROM COMPUTER. You have a mother?

JENNY CHOW. Yes. She is very …

SU YANG. *(In Mandarin.) Xum me?*

VOICE TRANSLATOR FROM COMPUTER. Yes?

JENNY CHOW. She is very …

JENNIFER MARCUS. *(Into her watch. Pause.)* She loves me very much.

JENNY CHOW. She loves me very much. *(Su Yang begins to cry again.)*

SU YANG. *(In Mandarin.) Dui bu qi. Wo dui bu qi ni, dang shi wo zhen de mai ban fa. Dui bu qi.*

VOICE TRANSLATOR FROM COMPUTER. I am so sorry. I am so very sorry. I could not do anything for you. I am so sorry.

JENNIFER MARCUS. *(Into her watch.)* It's okay.

JENNY CHOW. O-kay. It is o-kay.

SU YANG. *(In Mandarin.) Wo dang shi tai hian qing. Wo hai mei*

... wo hai mei ... wo de fu mu ... wo bu neng liu zhu ni.

VOICE TRANSLATOR FROM COMPUTER. I was very young. I was not ... I was not ... There were some problems. My parents ... I could not keep you ...

JENNIFER MARCUS. *(Into her watch.)* Do I have a father? Is that my father inside, in the house? Is that my brother?

JENNY CHOW. Do I have father? In the house. Is that my father? My brother?

SU YANG. *(In Mandarin.) Oh bu. Bu bu bu. Hai zhi. Bu. Ni de fu qing. Ta bu shi ...*

VOICE TRANSLATOR FROM COMPUTER. Oh no. No. No. No. Little one. No. Your father. He was not ...

JENNIFER MARCUS. Yes?

JENNY CHOW. Yes.

SU YANG. *(In Mandarin.) Ta bu shi ge hao ren. Wo dang shi bu zhir dao. Dui bu qi.*

VOICE TRANSLATOR FROM COMPUTER. He was not a good man. I did not know him. I am so sorry. *(Jennifer falls back in her chair.)*

JENNY CHOW. I like to read books. I like to look at birds. I am a bird. I like to fly into the white clouds. I like to look down at houses. I like the shapes of farms.

SU YANG. *(In Mandarin.) Ni e ma?*

VOICE TRANSLATOR FROM COMPUTER. Are you hungry?

JENNY CHOW. I am hungry. *(We hear music, but it is not excitable. Su Yang goes back inside. She takes some dumplings from the table. She wraps them in the scarf. Mr. Zhang looks up from his newspaper, shakes his head. Su Yang goes back outside.)*

SU YANG. *(In Mandarin.) Zhe ge, ni na zhe.*

VOICE TRANSLATOR FROM COMPUTER. Here, you take this.

JENNY CHOW. Thank you.

SU YANG. *(In Mandarin.) Ni hen mei.*

VOICE TRANSLATOR FROM COMPUTER. You are very beautiful. *(Su Yang embraces Jenny Chow. Jennifer Marcus's body folds in, as if she can feel, thousands of miles away, her mother touching her.)*

MR. ZHANG. *(In Mandarin.) Su Yang!*

SU YANG. *(In Mandarin.) Wo dei jing que le. Ta bun eng zhi dao you ni.*

VOICE TRANSLATOR FROM COMPUTER. I have to go now. He does not know about you.

JENNY CHOW. I have to go.

SU YANG. *(In Mandarin.) Ni bi xu zhou, ta bu neng zhi dao you ni.*

VOICE TRANSLATOR FROM COMPUTER. You have to go. He cannot know about you.

JENNY CHOW. I have to go now.

SU YANG. *(In Mandarin.) Zhen dui bu qi.*

VOICE TRANSLATOR FROM COMPUTER. I am so sorry. *(Su Yang runs back into the house. Jenny Chow follows her to the door.)*

THE BOY. *(In Mandarin.) Ma, na shi shui?*

VOICE TRANSLATOR FROM COMPUTER. Mom, who is that?

SU YANG. *(In Mandarin.) Shi yao fan de hai zhi.*

VOICE TRANSLATOR FROM COMPUTER. Some beggar child. *(Su Yang shuts the door on Jenny Chow. Jennifer Marcus shuts off her translator. Lights down on Su Yang, Mr. Zhang, and the boy. Jenny Chow looks confused, maybe upset?)*

JENNIFER MARCUS. *(Into her watch.)* Come home, Jenny.

JENNY CHOW. Jennifer?

JENNIFER MARCUS. *(Into her watch.)* Yes, Jenny?

JENNY CHOW. *(Pause.)* Something has happened.

JENNIFER MARCUS. *(Into her watch. Pause.)* Come home, Jenny.

JENNY CHOW. What is beggar child?

JENNIFER MARCUS *(Into her watch. Pause.)* What? *(Pause.)* Oh. It's a … good thing.

JENNY CHOW. *(Pause.)* Are we happy?

JENNIFER MARCUS. *(Into her watch. Pause.)* We're fine.

JENNY CHOW. I am fine.

JENNIFER MARCUS. Come home, Jenny.

JENNY CHOW. Jenny come home. *(Jenny Chow exits. We hear a "swoosh" noise. Jennifer sits, alone for a moment.)*

TODD. *(Offstage.)* Jennifer! *(Todd enters, he is wearing a jacket and out of breath. Shouting up at her window.)* Jennifer!

JENNIFER MARCUS. What?

TODD. JENNIFER! *(Jennifer walks to her window. She looks down at Todd, very subdued.)*

JENNIFER MARCUS. Todd?

TODD. It's me!

JENNIFER MARCUS. What are you doing?

TODD. I got some totally bitchin' news! *(Music begins to fade.)*

JENNIFER MARCUS. What happened to your car?

TODD. Huh? Oh. Right. *(Laughing.)* Your dad was right. Totally caved in on me.

JENNIFER MARCUS. You ran here?

TODD. I wanna show you something.

JENNIFER MARCUS. Look, Todd this ... really isn't a good time ...

TODD. Okay, are you ready?

JENNIFER MARCUS. ... Yeah.

TODD. Alright. Check it out! *(He takes the prototype Rubik's Cube, thrusting it in the air. Proud.)* Huh!? How 'bout that, huh?!

JENNIFER MARCUS. What? *(He looks at the cube.)*

TODD. Ah, shit! Wait, I just had it. *(He closes his eyes and manipulates the cube.)*

JENNIFER MARCUS. *(Quietly.)* Todd ...

TODD. Just gimme a second.

JENNIFER MARCUS. *(Meekly.)* Todd ... *(We hear a pulsating sound. Todd holds up the cube.)*

TODD. *(Shouting.)* Look! C'mon. Huh. It's all green! *(Jennifer tries to smile for him. The pulsating sound stops. Through clenched teeth.)* Motherfucker. *(He starts manipulating it again.)* Wait. Hold on a second. *(The pulsating sound returns. He shows Jennifer. Thrilled.)* Look, blue! Can you fucking believe it!

JENNIFER MARCUS. *(Quietly.)* That's really great, Todd.

TODD. I can do it! I can do it, Jennifer! *(The pulsating sound stops. Mr. Marcus enters.)*

MR. MARCUS. Todd? Is that you out there?

TODD. *(Shouting.)* Oh, hey, Mr. Marcus.

MR. MARCUS. What are you shouting about?

TODD. Well, actually, Mr. M. I'm going to Peru.

JENNIFER MARCUS. What?

TODD. *(To Jennifer.)* Yeah, uh ... Professor Nottage needs a driver.

JENNIFER MARCUS. *(Lost.)* Huh?

TODD. The woman who teaches the archeology class, someone backed out on her and she called me on the phone and you know, she said, "Hey, Todd. Wanna go into the field?" Can you believe that? I'm going into the field!

MR. MARCUS. When do you go?

TODD. We're going in like a couple of days. I got so much fucking stuff to do. Excuse the language, Mr. M.

JENNIFER MARCUS. Couple of days?

TODD. Yeah, it's like now or no way.

MR. MARCUS. What about your job?

TODD. Well, ya know, my car's trashed. *(Laughs.)* I guess, I've delivered my last pizza.

MR. MARCUS. Well, congratulations, Todd.

TODD. Thanks. *(He looks at Jennifer, then back at Mr. Marcus.)* Hey, uh, Mr. M. Would you mind? I just want to say something to Jennifer. Okay?

MR. MARCUS. Oh. Yeah. You bet. I'll just go back to my nap. *(Mr. Marcus exits.)*

JENNIFER MARCUS. Todd.

TODD. Alright, serious now. I want to tell you something.

JENNIFER MARCUS. Alright.

TODD. Look, I know, like we used to, well we used to like, like each other, right? And that never totally, worked out. But, I got to tell you something. Gimme a second, here. *(Pause.)* Look, I want to just say thanks.

JENNIFER MARCUS. Why?

TODD. Look, everyone totally blew me off after high school. And you're like, alright, this is not easy for me.

JENNIFER MARCUS. It's okay.

TODD. You are like the coolest person I've ever met. And it's been kinda weird 'cause you can't get out of the house and I like hanging out with you. Because you ... you make me feel like I can do *(Pause.)* anything I want to. And I really appreciate it. I don't think I'd be getting out of here if I didn't know you. *(Pause.)* Hey, how's Jenny Chow?

JENNIFER MARCUS. *(Quietly.)* She's good.

TODD. Good. *(Pause.)* Shit, man. I got a lot to do. Damn. I've got to get packed. I've got to get my emergency ...

JENNIFER MARCUS. ... emergency passport.

TODD. Yeah.

JENNIFER MARCUS. A travel visa.

TODD. A travel visa, right. I got so much to do. I hope I can do it.

JENNIFER MARCUS. I'm really happy for you. It's really great, Todd.

TODD. Yeah. Thanks. I'm gonna write, ya know. *(Music fades up. Jennifer nods. They stare at each other for a couple of moments. He starts manipulating the cube. After a second, we hear the pulsating sound again.)* Red.

JENNIFER MARCUS. Red. *(The pulsating sound stops. He looks up at her.)*

TODD. Peru!

JENNIFER MARCUS. *(As much volume as she can.)* Peru. *(Todd exits. She puts her hand up to wave goodbye. Lights change from day to twilight. We hear the sound of a car pulling up, a car door opening and closing.)*

ADELE HARTWICK. *(Offstage:)* Jennifer! *(Jennifer begins to hide all her "Jenny Chow" stuff. The goggles, etc. Offstage:)* Jennifer Marcus. *(When she thinks she's gotten everything in order, she walks downstairs. Offstage:)* Jennifer!

JENNIFER MARCUS. I'm coming. *(Adele enters with a briefcase. She puts it on the kitchen table. Music begins a slow fade.)*

ADELE HARTWICK. Hello.

JENNIFER MARCUS. Hi.

ADELE HARTWICK. You look like you've been crying.

JENNIFER MARCUS. Allergies.

ADELE HARTWICK. I brought you a gift.

JENNIFER MARCUS. Oh right … Thanks.

ADELE HARTWICK. It's a dress. I had a few hours and I found this terrific little dress in one of the stores. And I thought, wouldn't my little girl look great in that.

JENNIFER MARCUS. Thanks. Where is it?

ADELE HARTWICK. Where is it? Oh, it's outside. It's out by the garage.

JENNIFER MARCUS. Why is it out …

ADELE HARTWICK. Oh, I think you know why.

JENNIFER MARCUS. I forgot.

ADELE HARTWICK. What day is it, Jennifer?

JENNIFER MARCUS. I didn't do it on purpose.

ADELE HARTWICK. It's Tuesday. That means trash down to the street.

JENNIFER MARCUS. Mom. I'm really having a hard night and …

ADELE HARTWICK. You can't imagine what it's like having you as a daughter.

JENNIFER MARCUS. I'll do it in the morning.

ADELE HARTWICK. Bullcrap. The truck comes at five AM, Jennifer. When was the last time you got up at five AM?

JENNIFER MARCUS. I'll set my alarm.

ADELE HARTWICK. When was the last time you got up before noon?

JENNIFER MARCUS. Mom?

ADELE HARTWICK. I spent four hundred dollars on the dress for you, Jennifer. It's really beautiful. Little black thing. So perfect for you. I really think you're going to love it.

JENNIFER MARCUS. Then why didn't you bring it inside?

ADELE HARTWICK. Because it was a reward gift. And I came home and I saw that there was no reason to reward you, Jennifer. So I got mad for a second. I got mad out there because I promised myself I wouldn't do that in front of you. Because I'm trying, Jennifer. One of us is trying.

JENNIFER MARCUS. What do you want me to do? *(Adele walks to the front door, opens it.)*

ADELE HARTWICK. I want you to go outside by the garage, take all the cans down to the street and when you're finished …

JENNIFER MARCUS. I can't do that.

ADELE HARTWICK. … you can get the dress and you can try it on for me. Or you can try it on tomorrow. It doesn't really matter now. What matters is that you pull your weight around here.

JENNIFER MARCUS. I can't do it.

ADELE HARTWICK. What matters is that you keep trying. What matters, Jennifer, is that you actually get your shit together and do the one thing I ask you to do. *(Adele goes to Jennifer and begins walking her towards the front door.)* The one simple thing that assures me I don't have an invalid for a daughter.

JENNIFER MARCUS. I can't do it.

ADELE HARTWICK. No. You *won't* do it. *(Jennifer tries to free herself from Adele.)* No. No.

JENNIFER MARCUS. Let me go!

ADELE HARTWICK. No. No. You're going to do this.

JENNIFER MARCUS. Mom, please.

ADELE HARTWICK. So stubborn.

JENNIFER MARCUS. Please, Mom.

ADELE HARTWICK. You are going to take the GODDAMN GARBAGE out to the street, GODDAMNIT, JENNIFER.

JENNIFER MARCUS. Noooooo! Pleaseeee! *(Adele shoves her out the front door and shuts it behind her. Adele puts her weight against the door. Jennifer is frozen in fear on the other side, breathing heavily.)*

ADELE HARTWICK. I WILL NOT LIVE IN CHAOS, JENNIFER!

JENNIFER MARCUS. Please. Please. Please.

ADELE HARTWICK. I cannot come back to a house in chaos.

JENNIFER MARCUS. Please. I can't. Please.

ADELE HARTWICK. I need you to try, Jennifer. I need you to try. *(Mr. Marcus enters. Jennifer slides down the door.)*

JENNIFER MARCUS. Mom. Mom. Mom.

MR. MARCUS. What's going on, Adele?

ADELE HARTWICK. I got her a dress.

JENNIFER MARCUS. Mom. Please.

ADELE HARTWICK. She's just going to get the dress, Mark. *(Jennifer can't form words anymore. Mr. Marcus moves towards the door.)*

MR. MARCUS. Adele …

ADELE HARTWICK. She has to get her dress, Mark. I got her this dress.

MR. MARCUS. Get out of the way. *(Adele drops to the floor, still against the door.)* I need to get her, Adele.

ADELE HARTWICK. We have to help her, Mark. *(Mr. Marcus moves Adele out of the way.)* She needs our help, Mark. *(Mr. Marcus opens the door. He picks up Jennifer, carrying her inside.)* DON'T. You have to help. *(Jennifer shoves Mr. Marcus, then runs up to her room. Music fades up.)*

MR. MARCUS. *(Angry.)* WHAT WERE YOU THINKING? *(Lights out on Adele and Mr. Marcus. Jennifer sprays her body with disinfectant, then she starts tearing down all her blueprints, trashing her room, muttering to herself. She paces. A slow light change, from twilight to night, giving the impression she's been pacing for hours. She picks up a brush and starts combing her hair like she's out to hurt herself. After a moment, we hear a "swoooooossssh" noise. Jennifer sets down the brush, without stopping her pacing. A moment later, Jenny Chow climbs through the window into the room, carrying the scarf.)*

JENNY CHOW. Jennifer.

JENNIFER MARCUS. What?! *(Jenny Chow holds out the scarf. Music begins a slow fade.)*

JENNY CHOW. Are you hungry?

JENNIFER MARCUS. No.

JENNY CHOW. You are walking fast.

JENNIFER MARCUS. Get out of my way.

JENNY CHOW. I went to Dongtai. I flew in clouds. I met Su Yang.

JENNIFER MARCUS. So what? Get out of my way! *(Jennifer Marcus shoves Jenny Chow across the room. Jenny Chow stabilizes herself and walks back to her original position.)*

JENNY CHOW. Why do you push me, Jennifer? *(Jennifer shoves Jenny again.)* What is wrong?

JENNIFER MARCUS. She hated you!

JENNY CHOW. Hate?

JENNIFER MARCUS. You scared her.

JENNY CHOW. Who?

JENNIFER MARCUS. She looked at your hideous face and she was scared. She heard you talk like an idiot and you scared her away. You failed. Your design sucks. *(Jennifer rips one of her blueprints in half. Jenny Chow holds out the scarf to Jennifer.)*

JENNY CHOW. Are you hungry?

JENNIFER MARCUS. No, I am not fucking hungry. *(Jennifer hits it out of Jenny Chow's hand.)*

JENNY CHOW. What is wrong?

JENNIFER MARCUS. What is wrong? Whatiswrong-whatiswrong? What is WRONG is that I've spent every fucking waking hour of the last four months, pouring my fucking heart into a fucking box. A fucking pit. That's what I did. So stupid, stupid, stupid ... *(Jennifer starts hitting herself with her fist as she continues to pace around the room. Every time she hits herself, Jenny flinches.)* Stupid, stupid ... See, see, see this is the fucking problem, the fucking problem with an accelerated education! And I can FUCKING vouch for that one. One.

JENNY CHOW. Don't do that.

JENNIFER MARCUS. See it starts when they see you get nothing but straight A's, that's the fucking problem. The fucking problem is we don't really have to be parents anymore DO WE? No. She's fine. No. She's great. No. She's so fine. She's so great. But she's not great! Not greatnot greatnot greatnot.

JENNY CHOW. Stop hurting.

JENNIFER MARCUS. *(Shouting.)* I mean God forbid, Mr. and Mrs. Marcus, we just leave Jennifer out there on the playground. I mean, right? Huh? I mean right, ya know? How could we do that? She has to come inside. She has to come inside. One.

JENNY CHOW. Can we dance again? I like to dance. *(She rips up another blueprint.)*

JENNIFER MARCUS. *(Manic.)* There's a flaw in the design. There's a fucking flaw. The flaw is you. Come inside, Jennifer. Come inside. You can't stay outside. The design is flawed.

JENNY CHOW. I went to Dongtai.

JENNIFER MARCUS. Shut up. Shut up. SHUT UP.

JENNY CHOW. You are angry.

JENNIFER MARCUS. Could you shut the fuck up, please.

JENNY CHOW. O-kay.

JENNIFER MARCUS. Okay. Okay. Okay. One. Okay. One.

Okay. One. One. One. One. One. Zero. One. Zero one. Zero. One. One. One One. Zero. Zero. Zero. Zero. Failed. You failed.

JENNY CHOW. Jennifer …

JENNIFER MARCUS. *(Into her watch.)* Hit yourself. *(Jenny Chow hits herself in the head. Jennifer stops pacing.)*

JENNY CHOW. Jennifer.

JENNIFER MARCUS. *(Into her watch.)* Hit yourself. *(Jenny Chow hits herself in the head again.)*

JENNY CHOW. Please.

JENNIFER MARCUS. *(Into her watch.)* Hit yourself. *(Jenny Chow hits herself again.)*

JENNY CHOW. Thank you.

JENNIFER MARCUS. Hit yourself harder! *(Jenny does.)*

JENNY CHOW. Thank you.

JENNIFER MARCUS. I am ugly.

JENNY CHOW. I am ugly.

JENNIFER MARCUS. *(Into her watch.)* I have a hideous, ugly, fucking face.

JENNY CHOW. I have a hideous, ugly, fucking face.

JENNIFER MARCUS. *(Into her watch.)* And people hate me because I am worthless and ugly and a bitch and retarded and obsessive and fucking stupid. The stupidest ever.

JENNY CHOW. And people hate me because I am worthless and ugly and a bitch and retarded …

JENNIFER MARCUS. *(Into the watch.)* Hit yourself. *(Jenny Chow hits herself in the head.)*

JENNY CHOW. Jennifer? *(Jenny picks up the scarf, then holds it out to Jennifer.)*

JENNIFER MARCUS. What?!

JENNY CHOW. *(Timidly.)* Are you hungry? *(Jennifer stares at her for a second. She takes off her watch. She takes the scarf from Jenny Chow, puts it on her desk, then hands Jenny the watch.)*

JENNIFER MARCUS. Go. Get out of here. Get out of my face.

JENNY CHOW. Jennifer? *(Jennifer takes the watch and fits it on Jenny Chow's wrist.)*

JENNIFER MARCUS. Go. Get the fuck out of here. *(Jenny Chow looks at the watch. Then looks back at Jennifer. Exploding.)* WHAT?

JENNY CHOW. I am confused.

JENNIFER MARCUS. That's because I made you. And you're only going to get more confused. GO. *(Jennifer points to the window.)* I do not want you in my room. You cannot be in my room.

(She sprays Jenny Chow with disinfectant.) GO. You have to go. You have to go outside. *(She sprays Jenny Chow with disinfectant.)* I have to stay inside. You have to go outside. *(Jenny Chow walks to the window. Music fades in.)* You are flawed. You have to go.

JENNY CHOW. I am sorry. I am so very sorry.

JENNIFER MARCUS. *(Pause.)* You have to go.

JENNY CHOW. I am very beautiful. *(Jenny Chow climbs out the window. We hear a "swooooshhh" sound. Jennifer sprays disinfectant at the window and all over the room, everywhere Jenny Chow has set foot. When she gets to the scarf, she stops spraying. She sets down the can and undoes the knot in the scarf. She picks up one of the dumplings her mother set inside. She takes a bite. The floodgates open. She takes another. She eats the rest of it. She gets another one, crams that into her mouth, begins to devour all of the dumplings. When she can't eat anymore, she stops and stares at the scarf. She picks it up, then goes to the window. Looks out everywhere. She goes to her computer, types.)*

JENNIFER MARCUS. Dr. Yakunin. *(She goes back to the window, then goes back to the computer. Types something in it.)* Dr. Yakunin. *(Again, she paces back to the window, back to the computer. Panic ensuing. Types again.)* Dr. Yakunin. *(Lights up on the back of Dr. Yakunin. He turns around in his chair. Jennifer is pacing back and forth from the computer.)*

DR. YAKUNIN. Yes, Jennifer. I'm here.

JENNIFER MARCUS. Dr. Yakunin?

DR. YAKUNIN. What is it, child?

JENNIFER MARCUS. I've done something very bad.

DR. YAKUNIN. What is it?

JENNIFER MARCUS. Dr. Yakunin. *(Pause.)* She's gone. Jenny's gone.

DR. YAKUNIN. Oh, child.

JENNIFER MARCUS. Dr. Yakunin.

DR. YAKUNIN. I might know someone. *(Blackout. Lights up slowly on Jennifer Marcus. She is sitting at her computer, she wears the scarf around her neck. She is spent, open, vulnerable. Still trying to force a smile.)*

JENNIFER MARCUS. *(To the audience.)* And that's how I got in touch with you. I don't have much more to tell you. I am sending you a final attachment. It's just a couple of pictures of Jenny and some other stuff. *(Pause.)* And a picture of me. *(We hear a "bling" from the computer. To the audience.)* I really, you know, need to get her back. Please. These past four months, a lot of things have happened. Things I didn't really mean to happen. I made a lot of mistakes. But she's not one of them. She's my … perfect girl. And she's been gone for three days now and I was, you know, a little out of control when she left. And I'm not anymore. I'm a lot better now. *(She starts brushing her hair. One, two, three on one side, one, two three on the other. She repeats it. She puts down the brush, types again. To the audience.)* She won't cause anyone harm but she's infinitely more complex than anything out there. And she's very afraid. I can feel her. I can feel her. *(She picks up the brush, exact same routine, then sprays the computer with disinfectant. To the audience.)* I can pay you anything you need. You've been a really good listener, so thanks. And if you could bring Jenny back to me, that would be really great. *(Picks up the brush again, exact same routine only one more repetition. Again, sprays the computer with disinfectant. To the audience.)* So yeah, while you're looking for Jenny, if you're ever in the neighborhood, right off the Calabasas exit, and you just want to stop by, you can, you know. Just call at the gate and I'll have them let you in. Even if you just want to say hi, I would really like that a lot. *(Pause.)* I'm usually here. *(Pause.)* Yours sincerely, Jennifer Marcus. *(We hear a "bling" noise from the computer. She closes the laptop computer. She starts brushing her hair again, same routine. Lights fade. We hear her brushing her hair in the dark for a moment. Then nothing.)*

End of Play

PROPERTY LIST

Phone
Cardboard boxes, mechanical parts, blueprints
Silk scarf (JENNIFER MARCUS)
Computer (JENNIFER MARCUS)
Spray can of disinfectant (JENNIFER MARCUS)
X-ray (JENNIFER MARCUS)
Voice-ID earpiece (JENNIFER MARCUS)
Gyroscope, tool kit (JENNIFER MARCUS)
Suitcase and cell phone (ADELE HARTWICK)
Floss, mouthwash (JENNIFER MARCUS)
Radio, binoculars, cell phone (MR. MARCUS)
Newspaper (MR. MARCUS)
Work documents (ADELE HARTWICK)
Headphones, Rubik's cube (TODD)
Hairbrush (JENNIFER MARCUS)
Mail with letter, birth certificate (TODD, ADELE HARTWICK)
Pizza box (TODD)
Pizza (JENNIFER MARCUS; MR. MARCUS)
Computer camera (JENNIFER MARCUS)
Prototype Rubik's cube, blanket (JENNIFER MARCUS)
Drink (ADELE HARTWICK)
Computer, camera (DR. YAKUNIN)
Telephone book (DR. YAKUNIN)
Pen (TODD)
Robotic arm (JENNIFER MARCUS)
Cardboard box (TODD)
Garbage can (ADELE HARTWICK)
Pizza box with writing, skateboard (TODD)
Books (JENNIFER MARCUS)
Egg scrambler (MR. MARCUS)
Checkers (JENNIFER MARCUS)
Report (DR. YAKUNIN)
Pom-poms (JENNIFER MARCUS)
Headset cell phone (TODD)
Gloves (JENNIFER MARCUS)
Goggles (JENNIFER MARCUS)
Watch (JENNIFER MARCUS)
Laptop, airplane phone (ADELE HARTWICK)
Newspaper (MR. ZHANG)

Dumplings (SU YANG)
Briefcase (ADELE HARTWICK)

SOUND EFFECTS

Noise from the computer
Doorbell
Phone ring
Background noise of Taco Bell in Shanghai
Door slam
Muffled rocket engine
Trees splintering, muffled crash, water splash
Swoosh
Pulsating sound
Car, car door